Integrated Disaster Risk Management

About the Series

Just the first one and one-half decades of this new century have witnessed a series of large-scale, unprecedented disasters in different regions of the globe, both natural and human-triggered, some conventional and others quite new. Unfortunately, this adds to the evidence of the urgent need to address such crises as time passes. It is now commonly accepted that disaster risk reduction (DRR) requires tackling the various factors that influence a society's vulnerability to disasters in an integrated and comprehensive way, and with due attention to the limited resources at our disposal. Thus, integrated disaster risk management (IDRiM) is essential. Success will require integration of disciplines, stakeholders, different levels of government, and of global, regional, national, local, and individual efforts. In any particular disaster-prone area, integration is also crucial in the long-enduring processes of managing risks and critical events before, during, and after disasters.

Although the need for integrated disaster risk management is widely recognized, there are still considerable gaps between theory and practice. Civil protection authorities; government agencies in charge of delineating economic, social, urban, or environmental policies; city planning, water and waste-disposal departments; health departments, and others often work independently and without consideration of the hazards in their own and adjacent territories or the risk to which they may be unintentionally subjecting their citizens. Typically, disaster and development tend to be in mutual conflict but should, and could, be creatively governed to harmonize both, thanks to technological innovation as well as the design of new institutions.

Thus, many questions on how to implement integrated disaster risk management in different contexts, across different hazards, and interrelated issues remain. Furthermore, the need to document and learn from successfully applied risk reduction initiatives, including the methodologies or processes used, the resources, the context, and other aspects are imperative to avoid duplication and the repetition of mistakes.

With a view to addressing the above concerns and issues, the International Society of Integrated Disaster Risk Management (IDRiM) was established in October 2009.

The main aim of the IDRiM Book Series is to promote knowledge transfer and dissemination of information on all aspects of IDRiM. This series will provide comprehensive coverage of topics and themes including dissemination of successful models for implementation of IDRiM and comparative case studies, innovative countermeasures for disaster risk reduction, and interdisciplinary research and education in real-world contexts in various geographic, climatic, political, cultural, and social systems.

More information about this series at http://www.springer.com/series/13465

Adam Rose

Defining and Measuring Economic Resilience from a Societal, Environmental and Security Perspective

Springer

Adam Rose
CREATE
University of Southern California
Los Angeles, CA, USA

ISSN 2509-7091 ISSN 2509-7105 (electronic)
Integrated Disaster Risk Management
ISBN 978-981-10-1532-8 ISBN 978-981-10-1533-5 (eBook)
DOI 10.1007/978-981-10-1533-5

Library of Congress Control Number: 2016959389

Printed on acid-free paper

This Springer imprint is published by Springer Nature
The registered company is Springer Nature Singapore Pte Ltd.
The registered company address is: 152 Beach Road, #22-06/08 Gateway East, Singapore 189721, Singapore

To my grandsons Kellan and Ben

Foreword to the IDRiM Book Series

In 2001, the International Institute for Applied Systems Analysis (IIASA) and the Disaster Prevention Research Institute (DPRI) joined hands in fostering a new, interdisciplinary area of integrated disaster risk management. That year, IIASA and DPRI initiated the IIASA–DPRI Integrated Disaster Risk Management Forum Series, which continued over 8 years, helping to build a scholarly network that eventually evolved into the formation of the International Society for Integrated Disaster Risk Management (IDRiM Society) in 2009. The launching of the society was promoted by many national and international organizations.

The volumes in the IDRiM Book Series are the continuation of a proud tradition of interdisciplinary research on integrated risk management that emanates from many scholars and practitioners around the world. In this foreword, we briefly summarize the contributions of some of the pioneers in this field. We have endeavored to be inclusive but realize that we have probably not identified all those worthy of mention. This foreword is not meant to be comprehensive but rather indicative of major contributions to the foundations of IDRiM. This research area is still in a continuous process of exploration and advancement, several of the outcomes of which will be published in this series.

Japan

Disaster Prevention Research Institute

The idea of framing disaster prevention in risk management terms was still embryonic even among academics in Japan when Kobe and its neighboring region were shaken by the Great Hanshin–Awaji Earthquake (GHQ) in 1995. For example, Okada (1985) established the importance of introducing a risk management approach to reduce flood and landslide disaster risks. Additionally, it was not until late 1994 that the Disaster Prevention Research Institute (DPRI) of Kyoto University

Table 1 Conventional disaster plan vs. 21st century integrated disaster planning and management

Reactive	Proactive
Emergency and crisis management	Risk mitigation plus preparedness approach
Countermeasure manual approach	Anticipatory/precautionary approach
Pre-determined planning (if known events)	Comprehensive policy-bundle approach
Sectoral countermeasure approach	Adaptive management approach
Top-down approach	Bottom-up approach

had reorganized to add a new cross-disciplinary division of Sogo Bosai, or "integrated disaster management."

The new division of DPRI undertook a strong initiative among both academics and disaster prevention professionals to substantiate what is meant by integrated disaster management and to communicate to society why it is needed and how it helps. Many of these efforts were based on evidence and lessons learned from the GHQ. Japan's disaster planning and management policy changed significantly thereafter. Table 1 contrasts the approaches before and after that cataclysmic event. The current approach stresses strategies that are proactive, anticipatory, precautionary, adaptive, participatory, and bottom-up. The rationale is that governments in Japan had been found to be of relatively little help immediately after a high-impact disaster. Lives in peril had more often been saved by the actions of individuals and community residents than by official governmental first responders.

To understand a significant change in disaster planning and management in Japan, one must understand the contrasts among Kyojo ("neighborhood or community self-reliance"), Jijo ("individual or household self-reliance"), and Kojo ("government assistance"). Realizing limitations in the government's capacity after a large-scale disaster, Japan has shifted more toward increasing both Kyojo and Jijo self-reliance roles, and to depend less on the former, which in the past was the major agent to mitigate disasters.

One of the additional lessons learned after the 1995 disaster was to address the need for a citizen-led participatory approach to disaster risk reduction before disasters, as well as for disaster recovery and revitalization after disasters.

International Collaboration

In 2001, the International Institute for Applied Systems Analysis (IIASA) and DPRI started to join hands in fostering a new disciplinary area of integrated disaster risk management. That year, IIASA and DPRI agreed to initiate the IIASA–DPRI Integrated Disaster Risk Management Forum Series. Eight annual forums were held under this initiative, helping to build a scholarly network that eventually evolved into the formation of the IDRiM Society in 2009.

These activities, which were designed to be cross-disciplinary and international, have seen synergistic developments. Japan's accumulated knowledge, led by DPRI, became merged with IIASA's extensive expertise and became connected with inputs from the USA, the UK, other parts of Europe, Asia, and other countries and regions.

Major Research Contributions

Among many, the following contributions merit mention:

Conceptual Models Developed and Shared for Integrated Disaster Risk Management Okada (2012) proposed systematic conceptual models for understanding the Machizukuri (citizen-led community management) approach. Figure 1 illustrates the multilayer common spaces (an extension of the concept of infrastructure) for a city, region, or neighborhood community as a living body (Okada 2004). This conceptual model has been found to be useful to address multilayer issues of integrated disaster risk management at various scales. For example, in the context of this diagram, Machizukuri is more appropriately applied on a neighborhood community scale rather than on a wider scale, such as a city or region. Applied to a neighborhood community in the context of a five-storied pagoda model, it starts with the fifth layer (daily life), followed by the fourth (land use and built environment) and the third (infrastructure). By comparison, Toshikeikaku (urban planning) focuses mainly on the fourth and third layers. Another point of contrast is that Machizukuri requires citizen involvement to induce attitudinal or behavioral change, while this issue is not essential for Toshikeikaku.

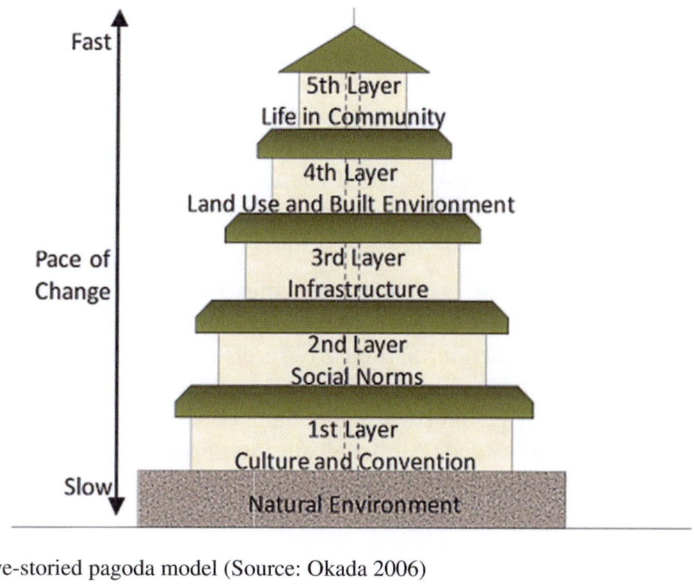

Fig. 1 Five-storied pagoda model (Source: Okada 2006)

Economic Modeling of Disaster Damage/Loss and Economic Resiliency Extensive research has been carried out by Tatano et al. (2004, 2007) and Tatano and Tsuchiya (2008) to model and analyze economic impacts of disruptions to lifelines and infrastructure systems caused by a large-scale disaster. For instance, simulating a hypothetical Tokai–Tonankai earthquake in Japan, a spatial computable general equilibrium (SCGE) model was constructed to integrate a transportation model that can estimate two types of interregional flows of freight movement and passenger trips. Kajitani and Tatano (2009) investigated a method for estimating the production capacity loss rate (PCLR) of industrial sectors damaged by a disaster to include resilience among manufacturing sectors. PCLR is fundamental information required to gain an understanding of economic losses caused by a disaster. In particular, this paper proposed a method of PCLR estimation that considered the two main causes of capacity losses as observed from past earthquake disasters, namely, damage to production facilities and disruption of lifeline systems. To achieve the quantitative estimation of PCLR, functional fragility curves for the relationship between production capacity, earthquake ground motion, and lifeline resilience factors for adjusting the impact of lifeline disruptions were adopted, while historical recovery curves were applied to damaged facilities.

Disaster Reduction-Oriented Community Workshop Methods The Cross-Road game developed by Yamori et al. (2007) proceeds as follows. During a game session, a group of five players read 10–20 episodes that are presented on cards one at a time. Each episode is derived from extensive focus group interviews of disaster veterans of the GHQ and describes a severe dilemma that the veterans of Kobe actually faced. Individual players are required to make an either/or decision (i.e., yes or no) between two conflicting alternatives in order to deal with the dilemma.

The Yonmenkaigi System Method (YSM) by Okada et al. (2013a, b) is a unique participatory decision- and action-taking workshop method. It is composed of four main steps: conducting a strength–weakness–opportunity–threat (SWOT) analysis, completing the Yonmenkaigi chart, debating, and presenting the group's action plan. The YSM is an implementation- and collaboration-oriented approach that incorporates the synergistic process of mutual learning, decision-making, and capacity building. It fosters small and modest breakthroughs and/or innovative strategy development. The YSM addresses issues of resource management and mobilization, as well as effective involvement and commitment by participants, and provides a strategic communication platform for participants.

Collaborative Research and Education Schemes Based on the Case Station-Field Campus (CASiFiCA) Scheme Acknowledging that diverse efforts have been made for disaster reduction, particularly in disaster-prone areas (countries), many professionals have been energetically and devotedly engaged in field work to reduce disaster risks. They recognize also that more community-based stakeholder-involved approaches are needed. A crucial question arises as to why we cannot

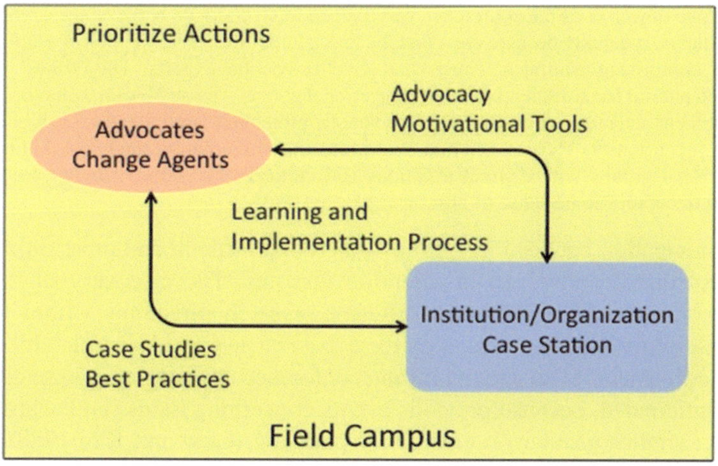

Fig. 2 Case Station-Field Campus scheme

conduct field work more creatively. One promising solution might be the CASiFiCA scheme originally proposed by Okada and Tatano (2008). As diagrammed in Fig. 2, the CASiFiCA scheme is characterized by a set of local case stations and field campuses and their globally networked linkages that are expected to operate synergistically to achieve the following objectives: promotion of IDRiM education at all levels, multilateral knowledge sharing and knowledge creation, and implementation of knowledge and gaining knowledge from implementation.

Europe

Integration via Regulation: European Union Experience

The integrated risk management of technological and natural hazard-triggered technological accidents (known as Natechs) has been a major theme addressed during the IIASA–DPRI Integrated Disaster Risk Management Forum Series since the first forum in 2001. In 2007 and 2008, the forum was hosted by the Major Accident Hazards Bureau at the Joint Research Centre of the European Commission in Italy, further strengthening the need for integration across natural and technological disaster risk management.

Integration was not (and, generally, still now *is not*) a self-evident concept when the first European Union Conference on Natural Risk and Civil Protection was launched in 1993, in Belgirate, Italy (Horlick-Jones et al. 1995). As the rapporteur-general wondered:

> Whilst one objective of the conference was to encourage dialogue between researchers and practitioners, it quickly became clear that the group structure was rather more complex than simply comprising natural scientists and civil protection experts. The 'tribes' present included natural hazard scientists, civil protection theorists – mostly social, behavioural and management scientists, industrial risk specialists, protection administrators and civil protection practitioners. The hazards and civil protection 'community' included a number of professional groups with distinct traditions and cultures. The term 'tribe' is used in an attempt to capture some sense of how strong is this divide.

Communication between the groups was rather difficult and most surprising for people not directly involved in scientific disputes. The discovery of the strong opposing views existing between different research directions within the same "hard" discipline (e.g., in seismology the debate on earthquake predictability) made even the agreement on an agenda for the conference challenging. These difficulties were unanticipated, because previous events concerning industrial hazards—organized in a similar manner on emergency planning (Gow and Kay 1988) and risk communication (Gow and Otway 1990)—found a rather cooperative atmosphere.

Despite the fact that the organization of the conference involved three directorate-generals of the European Commission (Research and Education, Environment, and Joint Research Center), natural hazards activities were not covered by an institutional legal basis. Also, at the time, there was no mutual assistance/compensation agreement in the case of a natural disaster, but only an initial exchange of experiences among emergency response services of EU member states. On the other hand, the existence of a sound regulatory process that obliged the different actors to be involved in the risk management framework was the reason for the successful cooperation in the latter mentioned events.

The new regulatory process for chemical accident prevention is an example. The process was reactive rather than anticipatory. It was triggered by a number of major accidents—e.g., the dioxin release at Seveso (Italy) in 1976 and the explosion at Flixborough (UK) in 1974. These had in common the features that local authorities did not know what chemicals were involved and in what quantities. They did not know enough about the processes to understand what chemicals/energy could be produced or released under accident conditions, and there was a general lack of planning for emergencies. Given this background, the first 1982 Seveso I Directive (82/501/EEC) was largely concerned with the generation and the control of an adequate and sufficient information flow among the different actors in the risk management process (Otway and Amendola 1989). This covered industrial activities that handle hazardous materials and introduced an integrated risk management scheme with identification of the actors and their obligations (control/licensing authorities—operators) or rights to know (the public). It requires that potential major accidents involving hazardous materials be identified, adequate safety measure be taken to prevent them, and on-site emergency plans be implemented. The competent authorities (CAs) have to control the adequacy of such measures and provide for external emergency plans. The public should be "actively" informed of the safety measures and how to behave in the event of an accident. The operator is required to report any major accident to the CAs, and the CAs have to notify the European Commission, which keeps a register of accidents so that member states can benefit from this experience for the purposes of prevention of future accidents.

The Seveso I Directive was the background for further discussions at the international level, such as the Organisation for Economic Co-operation and Development (OECD) and the United Nations Economic Commission for Europe (UNECE), which resulted in further recommendations and conventions on trans-boundary effects related to major accidents (United Nations 1992).

Reacting to the tragedy in Bhopal, India and other issues identified during its implementation, the need for a revision was identified, particularly concerning the lack of provisions for land-use planning (De Marchi and Ravetz 1999), resulting in the Seveso II Directive (96/82/EC). It completed the transparency process, beginning with the obligation of disseminating information to the public on how to behave in case of an accident, and, in a relatively short time, changed the "secrecy" in most countries surrounded by chemical risks into unprecedented transparency (for the "evolutionary construction of a regulatory system" for an extensive discussion of all Seveso II requirements, see Amendola and Cassidy 1999). It established that the public should be consulted for land-use planning and emergency planning with respect to accident risks and therefore should be more directly involved in risk management decisions. Furthermore, the safety report and accident reporting systems became accessible by the public.

The Seveso II Directive focused much more on the socio-organizational aspects of the control policy:

- The concept of an industrial *establishment* was introduced, characterized by the presence of dangerous substances. The focus is on the interrelations among installations within such an establishment, especially those related to organization and management. Further, attention is given to situations liable to provoke so-called *domino effects* between neighboring establishments. This led to integrated assessments of industrial areas. Furthermore, it implicitly called for the analysis of external threats, such as natural hazards.
- The socio-organizational aspects of an establishment were strongly affected by the introduction of the obligation for a major accident prevention policy (MAPP), to be implemented by means of safety management systems (SMS) (Mitchison and Porter 1999). These provisions were introduced after the awareness that most of the major accidents of which the commission was notified over the years under the major accident reporting system (MARS) had root causes in faults of the management process (Drogaris 1993).
- The introduction of the obligation for a *land-use planning policy* with respect to major accident hazards has had important socio-organizational consequences, as a broader body of authorities, especially those dealing with local urban planning, are becoming involved in decisions about the compatibility of new development with respect to existing land use (Christou et al. 1999). This has been integrated with the requirement that the public shall be consulted in the decision-making process. This has also led to integration of planning policies with respect to other kinds of hazards, such as natural ones, assuring that appropriate distances are

kept between establishments, residential areas, and areas of particular "natural sensitivity."

- The provisions for *emergency planning* and *public information* have been reinforced, as the *safety report* becomes a public document, and the public must be consulted in the preparation of emergency plans.

The Seveso II Directive also approached management as a continuous process, because it did not limit the regulatory action to providing a license or a permit to operate. Instead it assigned the obligation to the operator to adopt management systems as a continuous process for feedback in the procedures relating to operating experience and managing the changes over time. Also, land-use planning addresses not only "siting" a new establishment but also considers the compatibility of major changes with the existing environment as well as the control of urbanization around an establishment. Furthermore, it promoted common efforts among authorities, operators, and risk analysts to improve the risk assessment procedures and achieve better risk governance processes (Amendola 2001).

As mentioned above, the Seveso II Directive called for the analysis of external hazards as part of the hazard assessment process. Both domino effects and land-use controls are of particular importance when addressing the risk reduction of chemical accidents triggered by external natural hazard events (Natechs). In fact domino effects may be more likely during natural disasters than during normal plant operation (Cruz et al. 2006; Lindell and Perry 1997). Their likelihood will depend on the proximity of vulnerable units containing hazardous substances, and the consequences will undoubtedly increase with the proximity of residential areas. The European Commission published guidelines to help member states fulfill the requirements of the Seveso II Directive (see Papadakis and Amendola 1997; Mitchison and Porter 1998; Christou and Porter 1999). However, the guidelines do not provide specific actions or methodologies that should be taken to prevent, mitigate, or respond to Natechs (Cruz et al. 2006).

In 2012, the European Commission published the Seveso III Directive, which amended and subsequently repealed the Seveso II Directive. The major changes included in the Seveso III Directive included strengthening of a number of areas such as public access to information and standards of inspections. Furthermore, the latest amendment now explicitly addresses Natech risks and requires that environmental hazards, such as floods and earthquakes, be routinely identified and evaluated in an industrial establishment's safety report (Krausmann 2016).

International Institute for Applied Systems Analysis (IIASA)

"Risk" has been part of IIASA's activity profile since the institute's foundation. This theme is critical, as the prospect of unintended consequences from technological, environmental, and social policies continues to stir intense debates that shape the future of societies across the world. Relying on probability calculations, risk became a theoretical focus designed to bolster a scientific, mathematically based approach toward uncertainty and risk management.

Early controversies in the 1970s and 1980s on nuclear power, liquid natural gas storage, and hazardous waste disposal—all early research topics at IIASA—made clear to the expert community, however, that probabilistic calculations of risk, although essential to the debates, are not sufficient to settle issues of public acceptance. In response, IIASA has pioneered research on risk perception (Otway and Thomas 1982), objective versus subjective assessments (Kunreuther and Linnerooth 1982), systemic cultural biases (Thompson 1990), and risk and fairness (Linnerooth-Bayer 1999).

As a critical part of this history, IIASA is widely recognized for its advances in stochastic and dynamic systems optimization (e.g., Ermoliev 1988), treating endogenous uncertainty and catastrophic risks in decision-making processes (reviewed in Amendola et al. 2013) and advancing statistical methods for probabilistic assessment (e.g., Pflug and Roemisch 2007). The hallmark of IIASA's risk research is the integration of these multiple strands of mathematical and social science research.

One important in-house model taking an integrated perspective in the RISK program at IIASA is the so-called Catastrophe Simulation (CatSim) Model, which focuses on the government and its fiscal risk in the face of natural disaster events. It is a mainstay of the program's methodological and policy research and was first developed to aid public officials in developing countries to assess catastrophic risks from natural hazards and analyze options to enhance their country's financial resiliency. The model takes a "systems approach" by integrating catastrophe risk modeling with financial and economic modeling. It enables users to explore the impact of traditional and novel financial instruments, including reinsurance and catastrophe bonds, in terms of the costs of reducing the risk of a financing gap. CatSim has proven useful in other contexts as well, e.g., for allocating climate adaptation and development funds to support disaster resilience in the most vulnerable countries. Based on the model framework, assessed exposure and financial vulnerability to extreme weather events on the global scale can be performed as well (Hochrainer-Stigler et al. 2014).

Beyond modeling, IIASA has pioneered the exploration of novel financing instruments to provide safety nets to vulnerable communities and governments facing climate risks (Linnerooth-Bayer and Amendola 2000). These instruments now feature prominently on the agendas of development organizations and NGOs, and they are also gaining attention in the climate change adaptation community (Linnerooth-Bayer and Hochrainer-Stigler 2015). In an early influential policy paper, IIASA scientists argued that donor-supported risk-transfer programs, some based on novel instruments, would leverage limited disaster-aid budgets and free recipient countries from depending on the vagaries of post-disaster assistance (Linnerooth-Bayer et al. 2005).

As a final mention, IIASA's contributions to integrated disaster risk management have included the design and implementation of new forms of bottom-up governance, most notably stakeholder processes which co-design policy options with experts and explicitly recognize large value differences.

The USA

Multidisciplinary Center for Earthquake Engineering Research

The National Center for Earthquake Engineering Research (NCEER) was established at the State University of New York at Buffalo in 1986, with funding from the US National Science Foundation (NSF), the state of New York, and industrial partners. NCEER's original vision focused on multidisciplinary research and education aimed at reducing earthquake losses. Although the Center's main priority was to support research in structural, civil, and geotechnical engineering, it also provided funding for research in the fields of economics, urban planning, regional science, and sociology. Despite NCEER's ambitious vision, much of the research conducted during the 10-year period of initial grant support remained discipline-specific, although with the passage of time there was greater integration across disciplines, particularly in areas such as earthquake loss estimation, which required collaborative approaches.

When NCEER leaders decided to enter a new competition for NSF funding in the mid-1990s, there was general agreement that investigators should step up their multidisciplinary collaborative efforts based on an understanding that earthquake risk reduction and risk management require contributions from a range of areas of expertise beyond traditional engineering fields. This was made explicit when the leadership decided to change the Center's name to the Multidisciplinary Center for Earthquake Engineering Research (MCEER). Participation in multidisciplinary teams was strongly encouraged as MCEER investigators increasingly tackled problems that were beyond the scope of individual disciplines. Experts in remote sensing and in structural engineering worked together on the development of building inventories and, later on, rapid post-earthquake damage assessment methods using remotely sensed data. Engineers, economists, and sociologists worked on improving earthquake loss estimation methods, focusing, for example, on estimating potential damage to urban lifeline systems as well as resulting direct and indirect economic losses. Collaborating teams developed earthquake recovery models and explored the economic, political, and institutional obstacles that stand in the way of adopting and implementing risk reduction policy. Researchers studied hospitals both as critical physical systems and as organizations. A multidisciplinary group consisting of engineers, policy experts, and decision scientists developed decision-support tools designed to help facility owners make informed choices about alternative seismic risk reduction measures.

In the late 1990s, another team of researchers from various fields began a series of projects focused on the conceptualization and measurement of earthquake (and general disaster) resilience. Recognizing that resilience itself is a multidisciplinary and even a transdisciplinary concept, researchers surveyed a wide range of studies in fields ranging from ecology to psychology, identified common concepts and indicators, and developed one of the first frameworks that applied the resilience concept to natural hazards. One early product resulting from that collaboration was the article "A Framework to Quantitatively Assess and Enhance the Seismic Resilience of

Communities" (Bruneau et al. 2003). Authors of that paper represented the fields of civil, geotechnical, and structural engineering, operations research, economic geography, decision science, and sociology.

These successful collaborations were the result of several factors. Research activities were problem focused, and the researchers involved recognized that the earthquake problem is multidimensional. Methodological tools such as geographic information systems were useful in bringing about integration across disciplines. The longevity of NCEER and MCEER was also important; long-term funding made it possible for investigators to engage with one another over prolonged periods. This also meant that over time, researchers came to better understand and appreciate the approaches and methods employed by their counterparts in other disciplines. Additionally, the intent of the funding source was a significant influence; NSF made it clear that it was looking for research that was capable of overcoming disciplinary silos.

A major example of integrated research at MCEER was the first New Madrid (Earthquake Zone) electricity lifeline case study (Shinozuka et al. 1998), which focused on the site of the largest earthquake to strike North America in its recorded history. The study team was composed of engineers, geographic information scientists, economists, regional scientists, planners, and sociologists. They addressed the complexity of the interaction of various systems in the Memphis Tennessee Metropolitan Area. This included the vulnerability of the lifeline network, business response to physical damage and production disruption, estimation of direct and indirect losses in the region and throughout the USA, and policy analysis and implementation. At the core of the research were models of economic, social, and spatial interdependence, such as input–output analysis, multisector mathematical programming, and social accounting matrices (all precursors of the now state-of-the-art approach of computable general equilibrium analysis). This research was performed around the same time as the development of FEMA's loss estimation software tool HAZUS (FEMA 1997, 2016), which was another example of an integrated assessment model (see also Whitman et al. 1997). The capabilities included in HAZUS had to be simplified in order to be incorporated into a decision-support system that could be used by a wide spectrum of emergency managers and analysts on a desktop PC. In contrast, the MCEER research was intended to advance the state of the art in improving the scope and accuracy of hazard loss estimation. As such, it proved valuable in future extensions and upgrades of HAZUS and informed other research and public and private decision-making. One of its major points was the prioritization of electricity service restoration according to various societal objectives such as minimizing lost production and employment. As one of the study authors noted: "Not taking advantage of such opportunities results in an outcome as devastating as if the earthquake actually toppled the buildings in which the lost production would've originated" (p. xvii).

MCEER was directed by Masanobu Shinozuka, George Lee and Michel Bruneau. Researchers who contributed to the integration of various disciplines under its umbrella, in addition to the directors, included Barclay Jones, Kathleen Tierney, Tom O'Rourke, Bill Petak, Charles Scawthorn, Detlof von Winterfeldt, Stephanie Chang, Ron Eguchi, and Adam Rose. Two sister centers of MCEER were established with NSF Funding in the mid-1990s: the Pacific Earthquake Engineering Center (PEER), headquartered at the University of California, Berkeley, with a focus on performance-based engineering; and the Mid-American Earthquake Center (MAE), headquartered at the University of Illinois, Urbana, with a focus on a multi-hazard approach to engineering.

Natural Hazards Center

The Natural Hazards Research and Applications Information Center at the University of Colorado Boulder—now called the Natural Hazards Center (NHC)—was founded in 1976 by Gilbert F. White, a geographer, and J. Eugene Haas, a sociologist. Center activities were built upon the foundation that White and his collaborators from many disciplines had already established, as outlined in the books *Natural Hazards: Local, National, and Global* (White 1976) and *Assessment of Research on Natural Hazards* (White and Haas 1975). In the *Assessment*, White and Haas argued that efforts to prevent and reduce disaster losses relied far too much on technological approaches, without taking into account research in the social sciences. Their position was that such research could offer important insights into societal responses to hazards and disasters while also shedding light on whether technological approaches aimed at reducing losses were likely to produce their intended outcomes. Early research assessments focused on "adjustments" to hazards that communities and societies can adopt either singly or in combination: relief and rehabilitation, insurance, warning systems, technological adjustments such as protective works, and land-use management. In the view of the founders, a key task for researchers was to better understand the conditions under which particular adjustments would be adopted and their subsequent impact on disaster losses. Early in its history, the NHC produced its own series of books, monographs, and special reports, many of which focused on findings from US National Science Foundation-sponsored research carried out by investigators in the social, economic, and policy sciences. That practice was discontinued as specialized journals began to proliferate and an increasing number of academic and commercial publishers began to show an interest in publishing research monographs and textbooks in the disaster field.

From its inception, the NHC has had a dual mission. First, it serves as a clearinghouse and information provider for social science research on hazard mitigation, preparedness, response, and recovery, again with an emphasis on alternative adjustments to hazards. The idea of an information clearinghouse arose out of recognition of the difficulties associated with getting research applied in real-world settings. Clearinghouse activities include the production and distribution of the NHC newsletter, the *Natural Hazards Observer,* library and information services, and the annual NHC workshop, which has grown over the years. From the beginning, the annual workshop was designed to bridge communication gaps among researchers and graduate students from a variety of physical, social science, and engineering disciplines, government decision-makers, and emergency management practitioners. The NHC also administers a small-grant quick-response research program that enables researchers and students to go into the field immediately following disasters and then publishes the results of those studies. Second, NHC faculty and graduate students conduct their own research, with support from the National Science Foundation and other sponsors.

Both the activities associated with the production of the original *Assessment* and subsequent center activities involved the training of young researchers from a variety of social science disciplines. The first generation of center graduate trainees included well-known researchers such as Harold Cochrane (economics); Eve Gruntfest and John Sorensen (geography); Dennis Mileti, Robert Bolin, and Patricia Bolton (sociology); and Michael Lindell (psychology).

During the 1990s, the NHC conducted the second assessment of research on natural hazards under the leadership of director Dennis Mileti. The second assessment, which involved contributions from approximately 120 researchers, students, agency personnel, and other public officials, resulted in five books and numerous published articles and reports, again reflecting a range of social science perspectives (e.g., Mileti 1999). Like its predecessor, the second assessment provided training for another generation of researchers.

Since the early 2000s, the NHC has been increasingly involved in multidisciplinary research projects. Examples include collaborations with computer scientists and other social scientists on new technologies for emergency management, with economists on post-disaster business and economic resilience, with researchers from the National Center for Atmospheric Research on warning systems, with investigators from a number of social science disciplines on homeland security-related issues, with engineering researchers on recovery from the 2004 Indian Ocean tsunami, and with engineers, earth scientists, and policy scientists on the problem of induced earthquakes.

The NHC has served under the able directions of its founders and successor directors geographer William Riebsame (now William Travis), sociologists Dennis Mileti and Kathleen Tierney, and, beginning in January 2017, sociologist Lori Peek.

Center for Risk and Economic Analysis of Terrorism Events (CREATE)

Soon after the September 11, 2001, terrorist attacks in the USA, the nation's National Academy of Sciences performed an assessment of how the scientific community, broadly defined, could contribute to reducing the terrorist threat. One of their recommendations was to establish university centers of excellence (COEs) in research and teaching. The first of these was the Center for Risk and Economic Analysis of Terrorism Events (CREATE), established in 2004 and headquartered at the University of Southern California but being a geographically distributed entity with more than a dozen affiliates at other universities and research organizations throughout the USA and some overseas. These faculty affiliates came from the

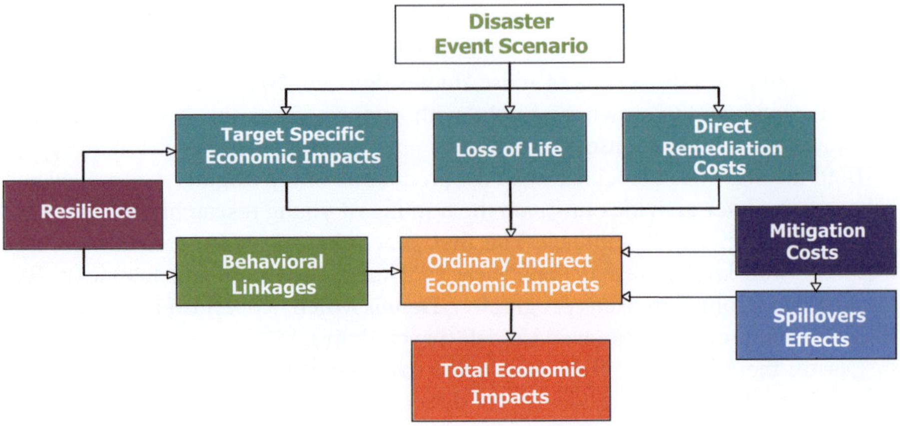

Fig. 3 CREATE economic consequence analysis framework

disciplines of decision analysis, risk analysis, psychology, economics, business, regional science, planning, operations research, public policy, public administration, public health, computer science, and communications. Founding directors were Randolph Hall and Detlof von Winterfeldt; subsequent directors were Stephen Hora and Ali Abbas, with von Winterfeldt returning after serving as director of IIASA.

Despite the restrictive nature of its title, CREATE was intended to be an "all hazards" center, although research in areas other than terrorism has been in the minority. CREATE was initially based on three themes: risk assessment, economic consequence analysis (and related topics in economics), and risk management. Risk communication was later inserted into the base of the framework. Much of the research has been multidisciplinary and some of it interdisciplinary.

One of the major interdisciplinary contributions was the development of a comprehensive framework for economic consequence analysis (ECA), as depicted in Fig. 3. This framework expanded ordinary economic impact analysis and hazard loss estimation substantially, first, by incorporating resilience. Building on his research at MCEER, Rose refined the concept of economic resilience into its static and dynamic versions, which are analyzed in the context of business interruption (BI), and focused the research on the demand, or customer, side, in terms of how businesses, households, and government agencies utilize remaining resources more efficiently and recover more quickly (see, e.g., Rose 2009 and this volume in the IDRiM Book Series). CREATE researchers performed many case studies using the operational metric that resilience effectiveness of any given strategy was equal to the averted BI as a proportion of the total potential BI in the absence of implementing the strategy. A major example was the finding that 72 % of the potential BI losses stemming from the destruction of the World Trade Center were averted by the rapid relocation of its business and government tenants (Rose et al. 2009).

Subsequent research has established the basis of an economic resilience index based on actionable variables (Rose and Krausmann 2013).

Another innovation was to incorporate "behavioral linkages," primarily off-site, post-disaster responses caused by such phenomena as the social amplification of risk and stigma effects. Many of these reactions are related to fear, as exemplified by the large BI following 9/11 from the decline of airline travel and related tourism (von Winterfeldt et al. 2006; Rose et al. 2009). A more in-depth and integrated analysis was undertaken to examine the BI losses from a simulated dirty bomb attack on the Los Angeles Financial District (Giesecke et al. 2012). This study examined the costs of potential wage and investor rate of return premia and customer discounts needed to attract people back to the targeted areas and inserted these costs in the state-of-the-art tool of economic consequence analysis—computable general equilibrium (CGE) modeling. The study results indicated that behavioral effects were 15 times larger than the ordinary direct and indirect economic impacts typically measured.

More recently, the framework has been "transitioned" to a user-friendly software tool known as E-CAT (Rose et al. 2017—a forthcoming volume in the IDRiM Book Series). A further extension of ECA on a parallel track to enhance the US government's terrorism risk assessment capability is being completed by Dixon and Rimmer (2016).

Other examples of interdisciplinary research at CREATE include work on adaptive adversaries, risk perceptions, risk messaging, and the value of information in risk management. This includes numerous case studies for academic and policy advising purposes that have been undertaken by CREATE researchers. One set of these has been the collaborative efforts between CREATE and the US Geological Survey (USGS) on analyzing disaster scenarios, such as a catastrophic earthquake, severe winter storm, tsunami, and massive cyber-disruption (see, e.g., Porter et al. 2011).

CREATE is one of a dozen COEs, with others involved in interdisciplinary research being the Consortium for the Study of Terrorism and Responses to Terrorism (START) and the Coastal Hazards Center. The centers have involved major researchers in the USA on both terrorism and natural hazards, such as Dennis Mileti, Kathleen Tierney, Susan Cutter, and Gavin Smith. An example of pioneering research is that on community resilience by Norris et al. (2008).

Low-Income Countries

It is difficult to pinpoint the beginning of academic research on natural hazards and disasters in low-income countries. The humanitarian system has deep historical roots, but the emergence of a humanitarian knowledge community is more recent and began to accelerate in the 1970s (Davey et al. 2013: 29). The 1970s and 1980s saw significant attention given to food emergencies and famine (Comité d'Information Sahel 1973; Sen 1981) and also to floods and cyclone impacts (White

1976). The rapid growth of academic research in the 1970s and 1980s was arguably driven by the greater visibility and political saliency of disasters such as the famines in the West African Sahel and Ethiopia, huge loss of life in Bangladesh due to cyclones, and deadly earthquakes in Guatemala and China (Kent 1983; Wisner and Gaillard 2009). However, it was only in what the British call "development studies" that disaster vulnerability became a core concern during this early period, with, for instance, Chamber's introduction of the concept of vulnerability in the context of "integrated rural poverty" (1983) and theme issues of the *Bulletin of the Institute of Development Studies* devoted to problems of seasonality and to food security and the environment (Lipton 1986; Leach and Davies 1991). The international, interdisciplinary journal *Disasters* was launched in 1976. Geographers, political economists, anthropologists, students of international relations, and community health specialists were among the early contributors. Epidemiologists and other public health researchers were active in defining disasters as a new focus of research at about the same time (de Ville de Goyet 1976); however, they worked alone or in small groups. The large academic center devoted to interdisciplinary, integrated approaches to understanding and managing disasters in low-income countries is a more recent development.

National Interdisciplinary Centers in the Global North

In the early twenty-first century, dedicated research centers now exist whose staff and collaborators span disciplines from the earth science and geoinformatics, social work, engineering, and public health to psychology, economics, sociology, politics, and geography, among others. Their approach is generally applied to and focused on the policy and practice of management of disaster prevention and risk reduction, warning, response and relief, and recovery. Two examples are the IRDR at University College London and IHRR at Durham University.

The Institute for Risk and Disaster Reduction (IRDR https://www.ucl.ac.uk/rdr) at University College London draws from a wide range of the University's institutes and departments, including the Institute for Global Health, Development Planning Unit in the Bartlett School of Architecture, Faculty of Engineering Sciences, the Leonard Cheshire Disability and Inclusive Development Centre, and departments of earth science and psychology, among many others. IRDR affiliates conduct research on the public perception of risk and how diverse societies deal with disaster, understanding health risks and pandemics, the study of extreme weather and the climate forcing of geological hazards, innovative design and construction, planning and design codes, and issues of resilience and recovery. One UCL partner with IRDR, the UCL Hazard Centre, has placed Ph.D. student researchers in nongovernmental development organizations (NGOs) in order to enhance NGO effectiveness (https://www.ucl.ac.uk/hazardcentre/ngo).

The Institute of Hazard, Risk and Resilience (IHRR https://www.dur.ac.uk/ihrr/) covers a similar range of research topics and also engages staff and research students across many disciplines at the University of Durham. IHRR plays a central role in the Earthquakes Without Frontiers research program in a number of countries in the Alpine–Himalayan Belt. This work involves earth scientists, social scientists, a historian, and a professor of social work and seeks to understand secondary earthquake hazards such as landslides, as well as risk governance and perception of earthquake risks by stakeholders at a number of scales (http://ewf.nerc.ac.uk/). IHRR researchers are also investigating such health aspects of disaster management as the effectiveness of respiratory protection during volcanic eruptions and economic questions such as how well small and medium enterprises recover from flooding.

International Centers

Because the elimination of poverty and promotion of security for people from food shortage, disease, and natural hazards are among the mandates of a number of UN organizations and international organizations, it is not surprising that research on integrated disaster risk reduction and management also takes place in these institutional homes. The World Bank and United Nations Development Programme (UNDP) are keenly aware of risk and are active on issues of human security (World Bank 2014; UNDP 2014). The World Health Organization (WHO) and the World Food Programme (WFP) also commission and conduct research on the early warning and management of epidemics and food emergencies, respectively (WHO 2016; WFP 2016). The Intergovernmental Panel on Climate Change (IPCC) has addressed the impacts of climate change on poor people in poor countries, particularly in its major report on climate-related disasters (IPCC 2012).

Also at the international scale, a good deal of the work of IIASA has been important in shaping policy and practice of risk management in low-income countries, for example, in the area of disaster insurance. The Center for Research on the Epidemiology of Disasters at the Catholic University of Louvain (CRED) in Belgium has evolved from a collector and repository of disaster data into a multifunctional academic institution that also produces occasional reports of relevance to integrated disaster risk management. One example is its 2016 report on poverty and disaster deaths (CRED 2016).

The International Council for Science has launched an initiative on the integrated study of disaster risk (http://www.irdrinternational.org/). Based in Beijing, China, the program of Integrated Research on Disaster Risk (IRDR) is active worldwide, especially in the Global South. It encourages young scientists, and it is currently engaged in an international assessment of integrated research on disaster that may lead to the IRDR's becoming the hub of a community of practice for such work. Its other research areas include knowledge sharing on the assessment of disaster loss and of the factors involved in the ways that people make decisions regarding disaster risk. In all of these functions, the emphasis is on serving a networking and facilitating function among researchers.

Another major program at IRDR has been to develop a framework for the forensic analysis of disasters called Forin (IRDR 2015). It seeks to focus researchers' attention on the root causes of disaster that go beyond the physical triggering phenomena and simple human exposure. Forin is grounded in a theory of social construction of disaster risk (Wisner et al. 2004, 2016; Tierney 2014). While keenly aware of physical and biological processes that manifest as hazards, Forin focuses on the process of development itself as a locus of risk creation (Oliver-Smith et al. 2016).

The forensic approach of the IRDR's Forin framework is not unusual. For many researchers who come to disaster risk from a background of work on poverty and marginalization in low-income countries, disaster is understood as a manifestation of failed or distorted development (Lavell et al. 2012) and the accumulation of risk in everyday life (Bull-Kamanga et al. 2003). Data collected beginning in the early 1970s shows that marginalized and excluded social groups in formerly colonized and other low-income countries are more severely impacted by natural hazards (Wisner et al. 2004). Women die in greater numbers in floods and coastal storms. Small farmers and fishers end up losing their land and boats to more wealthy neighbors and money lenders and find it more difficult to reestablish viable livelihoods.

The perspective of research grounded in daily realities of the urban and rural poor has also revealed that local knowledge and ways of adapting to hazards have been overlooked by planners and managers. In the last two decades, there has been much research on how local knowledge of hazardous environments can be brought together with outside specialist knowledge (Wisner 1995, 2010, 2016). The concept and practice of community-based disaster risk management (CBDM) or risk reduction (CBDR) have become common among both academic researchers and a large number of nongovernmental organizations, and collaboration between civil society and academia has begun in this domain (Wisner et al. 2008; Kelman and Mercer 2014).

National and Regional Centers in the Global South

Interdisciplinary research is also being conducted by institutions within low- and medium-income countries themselves. In the Americas, the network of researchers known as La Red was a pioneer (http://www.desenredando.org/). Created in 1992, La Red has a relationship with FLACSO, the graduate faculty of social sciences shared by ten Latin American countries. La Red publishes a journal, *Sociedad y Desastres* (http://www.desenredando.org/public/revistas/dys/), suspended for a time, but now relaunched, and has incubated some of the world's most innovative work on participatory action research for disaster reduction and on deep analysis of the links between development and disaster. Many of these innovations, while originally focused on the region and published in Spanish, have taken on an international role in shaping how disaster is understood and measured. A disaster monitoring and inventory tool known as DesInventar (http://www.desinventar.org/) was created by associates of La Red. It makes use of sub-national media and civil society sources to catalogue small- and medium-scale hazard events that have been shown to have a major impact on livelihoods and human security. Since its earliest application in Colombia, it is now used in many parts of the world.

In South Africa, Stellenbosch University and North-West University have interdisciplinary centers devoted to disaster risk management. At Stellenbosch, the Research Alliance for Disaster Risk Reduction (RADAR) began in 2013 to build on 17 years of research and networking on the continent when the director was based at Cape Town University. A large body of work on urban disaster risks such as shack fires and risk management in South Africa has resulted, as well as work on flooding. In addition, Peri Peri University is coordinated from a base in RADAR (http://www.riskreductionafrica.org/partners-and-programmes/stellenbosch-university-stellenbosch-south-africa/). Peri Peri U is a network of 11 universities in sub-Saharan Africa that share knowledge on disaster-focused pedagogy and research methods. North-West University is home to the African Centre for Disaster Studies (ACDS http://acds.co.za/). Established in 2002, ACDS conducts research on disaster risk governance, gender and disasters, water-related risks, and climate change. It is also home to a peer-reviewed, open-access journal, *Jàmbá: Journal of Disaster Risk Studies* (http://www.jamba.org.za/index.php/jamba).

In South Asia, a group of researchers pulled from civil society, journalism, and academia produces the occasional *South Asia Disaster Report* (e.g., Practical Action 2010) coordinated by the NGO called Duryog Nivaran and facilitated over the years by the INGO, Practical Action.

Many of the participants in these various research efforts in the Asia-Pacific region, the Middle East, Africa, Latin America, and the Caribbean have collaborated over the years with research into local, lived realities of disaster risk and risk reduction. The Global Network of Civil Society Organisations for Disaster Reduction (GNDR www.gndr.org) has in this way been able to mount large surveys that involved 800 civil society organizations in 129 countries, tapping the knowledge of more than 85,000 respondents in its Views from the Frontline series (http://www.gndr.org/programmes/views-from-the-frontline/vfl-2013.html), as well as even more detailed studies of local risk perception and action in its Frontline and Action at the Frontline series (Gibson and Wisner 2016).

Summary

The examples provided above are not exhaustive. Groups of researchers in many universities, civil society organizations, and government departments in low- and medium-income countries carry out work on disaster risk, albeit some of it more and some less integrated and interdisciplinary, given differences in the history of relations among academia, news media, and government and differences in bureaucratic flexibility within higher education and government. The important takeaways from this brief overview are that:

- A vital and growing focus on disaster risk in low- and medium-income countries has emerged
- A consensus is growing that disaster risk in such countries is to a great degree a manifestation of failed development
- The applied focus on practice and policy leads such research toward an integrated management approach
- Systemic changes in governance and in the relations among academia, civil society (including the media), and government are necessary if research on integrated risk management is to flourish in low- and medium-income countries themselves, and elsewhere in the Global South, as opposed to relying primarily on work within rich-country institutions and international organizations in the Global North

Other Contributions

The brief summaries of research contributions on integrated disaster risk management presented above are not all-inclusive. They focus to a great extent on work performed through major research institutions. As such, they omit contributions by several who have contributed to the IDRiM cause before the formation of the organization and since. Some examples are noted below.

The interrelationship between disasters and development was given a significant boost by the establishment of a program in disaster and development studies at Northumbria University (UK) in 2000 (see also the Department of Geography/Disaster and Development Network, DDN). This also co-emerged with integration of more specialized fields such as health and well-being-centered disaster risk reduction and communities and resilience, all of which are based on integrated approaches. Early work by Andrew Collins and others focused specifically on infectious disease risk management, bringing together microbial ecology, socio-behavioral, and contextual analyses to identify best-integrated risk management practices in Mozambique and Bangladesh (see http://www.ukcds.org.uk/the-global-impact-of-uk-research/communities-against-disasters). A broader set of universities are involved in the UK Alliance for Disaster Research (UKADR) (www.ukadr.org).

In Austria, BOKU University has a long tradition in the research of water resources, including current involvement in the South East Europe (SEE) project CC-WARE (Mitigating Vulnerability of Water Resources Under Climate Change). It is led by the forest section of the Austrian Federal Ministry of Agriculture, Forestry, Environment and Water Management and includes 17 partners from 10 countries. The main objective of CC-WARE is the development of an integrated transnational strategy for water protection and mitigating water resources vulnerability as a basis for the implementation of national and regional action plans (http://www.ccware.eu/). See also Löschner et al. (2016).

DPRI, with funding from the government of Japan under its GCOE Human Security Engineering (HSE) initiative, promoted field-based research projects on disaster risk management in Asian megacities. The Mumbai project, 2009–2013, focusing on vulnerable hot-spot communities, was established with the objective of evolving scientific methodology on participatory grassroot-level disaster risk management. The project, a first of its kind in India and one among a few globally, was undertaken in collaboration with the Mumbai city government (MCGM); School of Planning and Architecture, New Delhi; the Tata Institute of Social Science; IIT Bombay; and JJ School of Architecture, Mumbai. One outcome is a breakthrough in process methodology that empowered the two hot-spot poor communities to play the lead role in what is known as community-based disaster risk management (CBDRM). IDRiM founding member Bijay Anand Misra served as the senior adviser and coordinator of the project (see Misra 2013).

IDRiM member Manas Chatterji has overlapped research on integrated disaster risk management with work on conflict management and peace science (see, e.g., Chatterji et al. 2012).

Several research centers working on aspects of integrated disaster risk management operate in Iran, such as the International Institute of Earthquake Engineering and Seismology, under the founding and long-term leadership of Professor Mohsen Ghafory-Ashtiany, who also serves as the Chairman of the SP Insurance Risk Management Institute.

As one major example of research in China, in 2011, the Risk Governance Group of the Chinese National Committee on International Dimensions Programme on Global Environmental Change (CNC-IHDP) launched its Integrated Risk Governance (IHDP-IRG) Project. As a ten-year international cooperative research effort, its mission is to improve the governance of new risks that exceed current human coping capacities by focusing on the transitions in and out of the occurrence of relevant risks in the global climate changes. Under this project Beijing Normal University, with the leadership of Peijun Shi and others, has led comprehensive scientific research that included the several case studies, a community risk governance model, and a proposed paradigm of catastrophe risk governance in China. See, e.g., Shi et al. (2013) for a comparative study of the Wenchuan Earthquake and Tangshan Earthquake, centering on hazard, exposure, disaster impacts and losses, disaster rescue and relief, and recovery and reconstruction.

Limitations of space restrict us from mentioning all those working on the topic of resilience, but, in addition to the people and organizations mentioned above, we note the following whose research is in the spirit of integrated disaster risk management: Erica Seville, co-Leader of the Resilient Organisations community in New Zealand, Stephane Hallegatte of the World Bank, and Swenja Surminski of the Overseas Development Institute.

Conclusion

Further efforts needed in the future to advance integrated disaster risk management include:

- Extending research perspectives and constructing new conceptual models
- Developing new methodologies
- Exploring yet uncovered and newly emerging phenomena and issues
- Engaging in proactive field studies in regions that face high disaster risks, but, where investigations have not yet been undertaken, performing field studies that incorporate research advances in disaster-stricken regions

Obviously, the above approaches are rather interdependent, and thus integrated disaster risk management is best promoted by combining them. For instance, emerging mega-disasters, which are caused by an extraordinary natural hazard taking place in highly interconnected societies, may require a combination of both the second and third points above, such as mega-disaster governance based in part on mathematical models of systemic risks. Also, long-range planning for societal implementation of integrated disaster risk management inevitably requires encompassing most of the above approaches.

The IDRiM Book Series as a whole intends to cover most of the aforementioned new research challenges.

Nishinomiya, Japan — Norio Okada
Milan, Italy — Aniello Amendola
Laxenburg, Austria — Joanne Bayer
Uji, Japan — Ana Maria Cruz
Laxenburg, Austria — Stefan Hochrainer
Los Angeles, CA, USA — Adam Rose
Boulder, CO, USA — Kathleen Tierney
Oberlin, OH, USA — Ben Wisner

References

Amendola A (2002) Recent paradigms for risk informed decision-making. Saf Sci 40(1–4):17–30

Amendola A, Cassidy K (eds) (1999) Special issue of the J Hazard Mater 65(1–2)

Amendola A, Ermolieva T, Linnerooth-Bayer J, Mechler R (eds) (2013) Integrated catastrophe risk modeling: supporting policy processes. Springer, Dordrecht

Bruneau M, Chang S, Eguchi R, Lee G, O'Rourke T, Reinhorn A, Shinozuka M, Tierney K, Wallace W, von Winterfeldt D (2003) A framework to quantitatively assess and enhance seismic resilience of communities. Earthq Spectra 19:733–752

Bull-Kamanga L, Diagne K, Lavell A, Leon E, Lerise F, MacGregor H, Maskrey A, Meshack M, Pelling M, Reid H, Sattertwaite D, Songsore J, Westgate K, Yitambe A (2003) From everyday hazards to disasters: the accumulation of risk in urban areas. Environ Urban 15(1):193–204

Chatterji M (ed) (2013) Cooperation for a peaceful and sustainable world, Part 1. Emerald Publishing, Bradford

Christou MD, Porter S (eds) (1999) Guidance on land use planning as required by Council Directive 96/82/EC (Seveso II). EC/JRC, Report EUR 18695 EN, Luxembourg.

Christou M, Amendola A, Smeder M (1999) The control of major accident hazards: the land-use planning issue. J Hazard Mater 65(1–2):151–178

Comité d'Information Sahel (1973) Qui se nourrit de la famine en Afrique? Maspero, Paris

CRED (Center for the Epidemiology of Disaster) (2016) Poverty and disaster deaths. Louvain, Belgium. http://cred.be/sites/default/files/CRED_Disaster_Mortality.pdf

Cruz AM, Steinberg LJ, Vetere-Arellano AL (2006) Emerging issues for Natech disaster risk management in Europe. J Risk Res 9(5):1–19

Davey E, Bolton J, Foley M (2013) A history of the humanitarian system. Humanitarian Working Group, Overseas Development Institute, London

De Marchi B, Ravetz JR (1999) Risk management and governance: post-normal approach. Futures 31(7):743–757

de Ville de Goyet C (1976) L' epidémiologie des désastres: Une science naissante au service des pays en voie de développement. Louvain Médical: Revue du Secteur des Sciences de la Santé de l'Université Catholique de Louvain 95:145–155 & 185–195

Dixon P, Rimmer M (2016) Economic implications of terrorism risk assessment scenarios: a dynamic computable general equilibrium analysis. Report to the U.S. Department of Homeland Security, forthcoming

Drogaris G (1993) Learning from major accidents involving dangerous substances. Saf Sci 16(2):89–113

Ermoliev Y (ed) (1988) Numerical techniques for stochastic optimization. Springer, New York

Federal Emergency Management Agency (1997) HAZUS. Washington, DC

Federal Emergency Management Agency (2016) HAZUS-MH. Washington, DC

Ghafory-Ashtiany M (2014) Earthquake risk of and risk reduction capacity building. In: Ismail-Zadeh A (ed) Extreme natural hazards, disaster risks and societal implications. Cambridge University Press, Cambridge

Gibson T, Wisner B (2016) Lets talk about you …: opening space for local experience, action and learning in disaster risk reduction. Disaster Prev Manag: An International Journal 25(5):664–684

Giesecke JA, Burns WJ, Barrett A, Bayrak E, Rose A, Slovic P, Suher M (2012) Assessment of the regional economic impacts of catastrophic events: CGE analysis of resource loss and behavioral effects of an RDD attack scenario. Risk Anal 32(4):583–600

Gow HBF, Kay RW (eds) (1988) Emergency planning for industrial hazards. Elsevier Applied Science, London and New York

Gow HBF, Otway H (eds) (1990) Communicating with the public about major accident hazards. Elsevier Applied Science, London and New York

Hochrainer-Stigler S, Mechler R, Pflug GC, Williges K (2014) Funding public adaptation to climate-related disasters. Estimates for a global fund. Global Environ Chang 25:87–96

Horlick-Jones T, Amendola A, Casale R (eds) (1995) Natural risk and civil protection. E&FN Spon, London

IPCC (Intergovernmental Panel on Climate Change) (2012) Special report on managing the risks of extreme events and disasters to advance climate change adaptation. Geneva. http://ipcc-wg2.gov/SREX/report/

IRDR (Integrated Research on Disaster Risk) (2015) The Forin project. Beijing, China. www.irdrinternational.org/wp…/03/FORIN-Case-Studies-Booklet-WEB-13-MB.pdf

Kajitani Y, Tatano H (2009) Estimation of lifeline resilience factors based on surveys of Japanese industries. Earthquake Spectra 25(4):755–776

Kent R (1983) Reflecting upon a decade of disasters: the evolving response of the international community. Int Aff 59(4):693–711

Krausmann E, Cruz AM, Salzano E (eds) (2016) Natech risk assessment and management: reducing the risk of natural-hazard impact on hazardous installations. Elsevier

Kunreuther H, Linnerooth-Bayer J (1983) Risk analysis and decision processes: the siting of liquefied energy gas facilities in four countries. Springer Verlag, Berlin

Lavell A, Gaillard JC, Wisner B, Saunders W, van Niekerk D (2012) National planning and disaster. In: Wisner B, Gaillard JC, Kelman I (eds) The Routledge handbook of hazards and disaster risk reduction. Routledge, London, p 617–628

Leach M, Davies R (eds) (1991) Food security and the environment. Theme issue, IDS Bulletin 22(3)

Lindell MK, Perry RW (1997) Hazardous materials releases in the Northridge earthquake: implications for seismic risk assessment. Risk Anal 17(2):147–156

Linnerooth-Bayer J (1999) Climate change and multiple views of fairness. In: Toth FL (ed) Fair weather? Equity concerns in climate change. Earthscan Publications Ltd., London, p 44–65

Linnerooth-Bayer J, Amendola A (2000) Global change, natural disasters and loss-sharing: issues of efficiency and equity. Geneva Pap Risk Insur Issues Pract 25:203

Linnerooth-Bayer J, Hochrainer-Stigler S (2015) Financial instruments for disaster risk management and climate change adaptation. Clim Chang 133(1):85–100

Lipton M (ed) (1986) Seasonality and ultrapoverty. Theme issue. IDS Bull 17(3):4–8

Löschner L, Herrnegger M, Apperl B, Senoner T, Seher W, Nachtnebel HP (2016) Flood risk, climate change and settlement development: a micro-scale assessment of Austrian municipalities. Reg Environ Change, forthcoming

Mileti D (1999) Disasters by design. Joseph Henry Press, Washington, DC

Misra, BA (2013) Disaster risk management: challenges and conflicts in 21st century governance, mega city Mumbai, in Disaster Risk Management Conflict and Cooperation, Concept Publishing Company

Mitchison N, Porter S (eds) (1999) Guidelines on a major accident prevention policy and safety management system, as required by Council Directive 96/82/EC (SEVESO II). EUR 18123 EN, JRC, Ispra

Norris F, Stevens S, Pfefferbaum V, Whyche K, Pfefferbaum R (2008) Community resilience as a metaphor, theory, set of capacities and strategy for disaster readiness. Am J Community Psychol 41:127–150

Okada N (1985) Putting disaster prevention into a perspective of risk management. Tsuchi to Bosai (Soils Management and Disaster Prevention), Japan Society for Civil Engineers

Okada N (2006) Perspective on integrated disaster risk management. In: Hagihara Y, Okada N, Tatano H (eds) Introduction to integrated disaster risk management. Kyoto University Academic Press, Kyoto, pp 9–54

Okada N (2012) Lessons learned from recent disasters in Japan, and implications for ASEAN countries. Keynote presentation at ASEAN-Japan meeting, Naha, 26 June 2013

Okada N, Tatano H (2008) Case Station-Field Campus (CASiFiCA): globally-networked, field-based research and education challenges for disaster reduction. Presented at IDRC DAVOS Conference 2008, Davos, Switzerland. https://idrc.info/fileadmin/user_upload/idrc/former_conferences/idrc2008/presentations/Program_forWebsite_V7.pdf#search='Davos+conference+Case+StationField+Campus+%28CASiFiCA%29+%3A+Globallynetworked%2C+Fieldbased+Research+and+Education+Challenges+for+Disaster+Reduction

Okada N, Fang L, Kilgour M (2013a) Community-based decision making in Japan. Group Decis Negot 22(1):45–52

Okada N, Na J, Fang L, Teratani A (2013b) The Yonmenkaigi system method: an implementation-oriented group decision support approach. Group Decis Negot 22(1):53–67

Oliver-Smith A, Alcántara-Ayala I, Burton I, Lavell A (2016) Forensic investigation of disasters: a conceptual framework and guide to research. Beijing. www.irdrinternational.org/wp-content/uploads/2016/01/FORIN-2-29022016.pdf

Otway H, Thomas K (1982) Reflections on risk perception and policy. Risk Anal 2:69–82

Papadakis GA, Amendola A (eds) (1997) Guidance on the preparation of a safety report to meet the requirements of Council Directive 96/82/EC (SEVESO II). EC/JRC, Report EUR 17690 EN, Luxembourg

Pflug G, Römisch W (2007) Modeling, measuring and managing risk. World Scientific, Singapore

Porter K, Jones L, Cox D, Goltz J, Hudnut K, Mileti D, Perry S et al. (2011) The ShakeOut scenario: a hypothetical Mw7. 8 earthquake on the southern San Andreas fault. Earthquake Spectra 27(2):239–261
Practical Action, Nivaran D (2010) South Asia disaster report 2010: changing climate, impeding risks, emerging perspectives. Colombo. http://practicalaction.org/disaster-report
Rose A (2009) Economic resilience to disasters. Community and Regional Resilience Institute (CARRI) Research Report Number 8
Rose A, Krausmann E (2013) An economic framework for the development of a resilience index for business recovery. Int J Disaster Risk Reduct 5:73–83
Rose A, Oladosu G, Lee B, Assay G (2009) The economic impacts of the September 11 terrorist attacks: a computable general equilibrium analysis. Peace Econ Peace Sci Publ Policy 15(2)
Rose A, Prager F, Chen Z, Chatterjee S, Wei D, Heatwole N, Warren E (2017) Economic consequence analysis of disasters: the E-CAT software tool. Springer, Tokyo, forthcoming
Sen A (1981) Poverty and famines. Oxford University Press, Oxford
Shi P, Jaeger C, Ye Q (2013) Integrated risk governance-science plan and case studies of large-scale disasters. Beijing Normal University Press/Springer, Heidelberg/Berlin
Shinozuka M, Rose A, Eguchi R (1998) Engineering and socioeconomic impacts of earthquakes: an analysis of electricity lifeline disruptions in the New Madrid Area. Multidisciplinary Center for Earthquake Engineering Research Buffalo, New York
Tatano H, Tsuchiya S (2008) A framework for economic loss estimation due to seismic transportation network disruption: a spatial computable general equilibrium approach. Nat Hazards 44(2):253–265
Tatano H et al (2004) Economic restoration after a catastrophic event: heterogeneous damage to infrastructure and capital and its effects on economic growth. J Nat Dis Sci 26(2):81–85
Tatano H, Tsuchiya S, Okada N (2007) Economic loss assessment due to railroad and highway disruptions. Econ Syst Res 19(2):147–162
Thompson M, Ellis R, Wildavsky A (1990) Cultural theory. Westview Press, Boulder
Tierney K (2014) The social roots of risk: producing disasters, promoting resilience. Stanford University Press, Stanford
UNDP (United Nations Development Programme) (2014) Human development report 2014: sustaining human progress: reducing vulnerabilities and building resilience. UNDP, New York
von Winterfeldt D, O'Sullivan TM (2006) Should we protect commercial airplanes against surface-to-air missile attacks by terrorists? Decis Anal 3(2):63–75
WFP (World Food Programme) (2016) Comprehensive food security and vulnerability analysis. https://www.wfp.org/food-security/assessments/comprehensive-food-security-vulnerability-analysis
White G (ed) (1976) Natural hazards: local, national, and global. Oxford University Press, New York
White G, Haas E (1975) Assessment of research on natural hazards. Cambridge, MIT Press
Whitman R et al (1997) Development of a national earthquake loss estimation methodology. Earthquake Spectra 13(4):643–661
WHO (World Health Organization) (2016) Early warning systems. http://www.who.int/csr/labepidemiology/projects/earlywarnsystem/en/
Wisner B (1995) Bridging "expert" and "local" knowledge for counter-disaster planning in urban South Africa. GeoJournal 37(3):337–348
Wisner B (2010) Climate change and cultural diversity. Int J Soc Sci 61(199):131–140
Wisner B (2016) Vulnerability as concept, model, metric and tool. In: Cutter S (ed) Oxford research encyclopedia of natural hazard science. Oxford University Press, New York. Online only: http://naturalhazardscience.oxfordre.com/view/10.1093/acrefore/9780199389407.001.0001/acrefore-9780199389407-e-25
Wisner B, Gaillard JC (2009) An introduction to neglected disasters. Jàmbá: J Dis Risk Studs 2(3):151–158

Wisner B, Blaikie P, Cannon T, Davis I (2004) At risk: natural hazards, people's vulnerability and disaster, 2nd edn. Routledge, London

Wisner B, Haghebaert B, Schaerer M, Arnold M (2008) Community risk assessment toolkit. ProVention Consortium, Geneva. Online only: http://www.proventionconsortium.net/?pageid=39

World Bank (2014) World development report 2014: risk and opportunity. World Bank, Washington, DC

Yamori K (2007) Disaster risk sense in Japan and gaming approach to risk communication. Int J Mass Emerg Dis 25(2):101–131

Preface

Resilience to disasters has become a popular buzzword over the past decade. Before that, its use had been on the increase but few bothered to define it (see, e.g., the absence of definitions in classic studies by Chernick 2005; Valle and Campanella 2005). Over the past 10 years, the pendulum has swung in the other direction, with dozens of definitions put forth for resilience in general and numerous ones offered for economic resilience in particular. Some of the definitions are so broad as to render the concept meaningless. There is concern that the high exposure and vagueness of the term will undercut interest in it and stifle its implementation.

The starting point of this volume is that economic resilience does not refer to every action that reduces economic losses from disasters, whether they are natural, man-made, or technological. There are perfectly good terms for what can be done to reduce losses in advance of the disaster, most notably interdiction and mitigation, which refer to reducing the frequency and magnitude of the initial shock, primarily with respect to averting property damage. What has been missing is a term to capture the various activities that can be used to reduce losses after the disaster strikes. Here the focus shifts from property damage to business interruption (typically measured in terms of gross domestic product or employment), which begins with the onset of the disaster and continues until the affected unit (household, business, industry, or entire economy) has recovered (or reached a "new normal"). Of course, resilience is also a process, whereby resilience capacity can be built up in anticipation of a disaster (e.g., stockpiling critical inputs, identifying alternative locations, conducting emergency management drills), but resilience tactics are not implemented until the disaster actually strikes. Thus, this definition is more in keeping with the original etymological root *resilio*, which means to rebound. In essence, I define static economic resilience as a process of using remaining resources more effectively, and dynamic economic resilience as investment in repair and reconstruction so as to recover at an accelerated pace. These concepts relate to classic definitions in the literature of maintaining function and recovering rapidly by Holling (1973) and Pimm (1984).

Overall, there are many more commonalities than differences in resilience definitions across fields such as planning, organizational behavior, sociology, ecology, and engineering. A major theme of this volume is how economic resilience relates to broader concepts of resilience from societal, environmental, and personal security perspectives.

This volume is the outgrowth of 20 years of research on resilience. My study of the topic dates back to the mid-1990s, before it came into fashion. I was fortunate to become a faculty affiliate of the National Center for Earthquake Engineering Research (NCEER), subsequently renamed the Multidisciplinary Center for Earthquake Engineering Research (MCEER), a U.S. National Science Foundation-funded research center, headquartered at the State University of New York at Buffalo. I was professor and head of the Department of Energy and Environmental Economics and then professor of Geography at The Pennsylvania State University during most of my association with MCEER. I worked closely with and learned greatly from: Kathleen Tierney, a pioneer in research on resilience, the concept of business interruption, and disaster recovery; Masanobu Shinozuka, a world leader in earthquake fragility analysis and former NCEER Director; Stephanie Chang, who has made major contributions to disaster loss estimation, resilience, and recovery; and Tom O'Rourke, a leader in earthquake engineering and someone who was always eager to reach out to social scientists. Others with whom I interacted included Barclay Jones, Hal Cochrane, Sam Cole, Ron Eguchi, Charles Scawthorn, Detlof von Winterfelt, and Michel Bruneau, as well as my graduate students at Penn State, including Juan Benavides, Dongsoon Lim, Debo Oladosu, Gauri Guha, Shu-Yi Liao, and Dan Wei. The classic paper by Bruneau et al. (2003) established a valuable multidisciplinary framework for the study of resilience. Still, I found that it omitted key elements of the economic dimension, which inspired me to set forth definitions and an operational metric (Rose 2004), formal modeling of economic resilience (Rose and Liao 2005), the identification of commonalities with other disciplines (Rose 2007), and efforts to measure resilience (e.g., Rose and Lim 2002).

My research on resilience received another boost when, in 2006, I moved to the University of Southern California (USC), with a joint appointment between the School of Policy Planning and Development (now the Price School of Public Policy) and the Center for Risk and Economic Analysis of Terrorism Events (CREATE), the first of now a dozen U.S. Department of Homeland Security (DHS) Centers of Excellence in Research and Education. With regard to CREATE's sister research center, Studies of Terrorism and Responses to Terrorism (START), I benefited from interaction with leaders in the fields of sociology (see a recent work by Kathleen Tierney 2014), social psychology (see the classic work by Fran Norris et al. 2008), and geography (see recent work by Susan Cutter 2016). Resilience was a major theme at first at both CREATE and START, although subsequently this support went through a cycle of favor, disfavor, and favor again by DHS. My research benefited from several years of funding support from the DHS Office of University Programs (OUP) and various other DHS offices and components (Office of Policy, Coast Guard, National Biosurveillance Integration Center, Domestic Nuclear Detection Office, and FEMA), as well as other DHS-funded entities such as the Community and Regional Resilience Institute (CARRI), on projects in which resilience was at the forefront or at least a key component of research on Economic Consequence

Analysis. I wish to thank DHS staff, most notably OUP Director Matt Clark and Program Managers Gia Harrigan and Bryan Roberts. This research also received the encouragement of CREATE Directors Detlof von Winterfelt, Steve Hora, and Ali Abbas, as well as CREATE Associate Director of Research Isaac Maya and Price School Dean Jack Knott and Senior Associate Dean for Research Gen Giuliano.

My research at USC extended to formal modeling of resilience at the micro level (Rose 2009a) and macro level (Rose 2015) and several case studies (e.g., Rose et al. 2007, 2011a, b, 2016; Rose and Wei 2013; Prager et al. 2016), including a definitive study of the economic consequences of the September 11, 2001, attacks on the World Trade Center, in which resilience played a major role in reducing losses (Rose et al. 2009). It also extended to the development of a resilience index (Rose and Krausmann 2013), and on the role of resilience in business interruption insurance (Rose and Huyck 2016). A major theme of my research was the development of an overall Economic Consequence Analysis framework in which resilience played a key role (Rose 2009b, 2015). This framework has been operationalized in a user-friendly decision-support tool known as E-CAT, which is the subject of yet another Springer IDRiM Series book (Rose et al. 2017).

More recently my research has focused on the collection of primary data to measure static and dynamic economic resilience, which has been funded by NSF and the new Critical Infrastructure Resilience Institute. In this research I have benefited from my interaction with my co-principal investigators, Kathleen Tierney, Noah Dormady, and Heather Rosoff. Over the past 10 years, I have learned much about resilience from my interaction with other researchers such as Dan Wei, Ian Sue Wing, Anne Wein, Amanda Bonneau, Elizabeth Krausmann, Charles Huyck, Stephen Flynn, Mark Ehlen, Eric Vugrin, Kurt Petersen, Phil Ganderton, Keith Porter, and Craig Taylor, as well as CREATE post-docs and grad students Bumsoo Lee, Fynnwin Prager, Zhenhua Chen, Jonathan Eyer, Misak Avetisyan, Noah Dormady, Phil Sczesniak, Noah Miller, Josh Banks, and Lee White. I have also benefited from interaction with practitioners such as Craig Davis of the Los Angeles Department of Water and Power, Lucy Jones of the U.S. Geological Survey, and Philip Schneider and Neil Blais of the National Institute of Building Sciences.

A sizable portion this manuscript emanates from an unpublished background report for the United Nations Development Programme (UNDP) Human Development Report 2015. This undertaking helped me further broaden my perspective in two areas of human development: personal security and societal resilience capacity (see especially Chaps. 1 and 7). I am grateful to Alan Fuchs for his support in this effort. More recently I contributed to a study sponsored by the World Bank and Overseas Development Institute on the co-benefits of disaster risk management, now also known as the "Resilience Triple-Dividend". My work on private sector co-benefits informs Chap. 9 of this volume. Here I am indebted to the guidance of Swenja Surminski and Stephan Hallegatte.

My research on resilience has also benefited from my involvement with the International Society for Integrated Disaster Risk Management (IDRiM). Resilience has been a major theme of this organization, which spans the range of conceptual research, empirical analysis, and policy implementation. I am grateful to colleagues such as Norio Okada, Hiro Tatano, Aniello Amandola, Ana Maria Cruz, and Joanne Linnerooth-Bayer for guiding the organization along this path and for their support of my efforts in terms of providing opportunities to disseminate my research at annual IDRiM conferences and through the Springer IDRiM Book Series.

My research on resilience could not have been achieved without the support of my devoted family over the years. Several family members have suffered my absences and inattention at many junctures. I especially single out my loving wife, Rebecca, who has given of herself in many ways to help me attain my professional goals. I will be forever grateful for all of her kindnesses.

My research on resilience has been inspired by the history of my near and extended family, which has been resilient for many hundreds of years, most recently as Holocaust survivors. This book is dedicated to all of them, but especially to my grandsons, Kellan and Ben, who I hope will not have the necessity of using this family capability to such an extreme degree during their lifetime.

Los Angeles, CA, USA Adam Rose

References

Bruneau M, Chang S, Eguchi, R, Lee G, O'Rourke T, Reinhorn A, Shinozuka M, Tierney K, Wallace W, von Winterfeldt D (2003) A framework to quantitatively assess and enhance seismic resilience of communities. Earthq Spectra 19:733–752

Chernick H (ed) (2005) Resilient city: the economic impact of 9/11. Russell Sage Foundation, New York

Cutter S (2016) The landscape of disaster resilience indicators in the USA. Nat Hazards 80:741–758

Ghafory-Ashtiany M (2014) Earthquake risk of and risk reduction capacity building. In: Ismail-Zadeh A (ed) Extreme natural hazards, disaster risks and societal implications. Cambridge University Press, Cambridge

Holling C (1973) Resilience and stability of ecological systems. Ann Rev Ecol Syst 4:1–23

Norris F, Stevens S, Pfefferbaum V, Whyche K, Pfefferbaum R (2008) Community resilience as a metaphor, theory, set of capacities and strategy for disaster readiness. Am J Community Psychol 41:127–150

Pimm SL (1984) The complexity and stability of ecosystems. Nature 307(5949):321–326

Prager F, Wei D, Rose (2016) A Total economic consequences of an influenza outbreak in the United States. Risk Anal, forthcoming

Rose A (2004) Economic principles, issues, and research priorities in natural hazard loss estimation. In: Okuyama Y, Chang S (eds) Modeling the spatial economic impacts of natural hazards. Springer, Heidelberg

Rose A (2007) Economic resilience to natural and man-made disasters: multidisciplinary origins and contextual dimensions. Environ Hazards 7(4):383–395

Rose A (2009a) Economic resilience to disasters. Community and Resilience Institute Research Report Number 8. ORNL

Rose A (2009b) A framework for analyzing and estimating the total economic impacts of a terrorist attack and natural disaster. J Homeland Secur Emerg Manag 6(1):6

Rose A (2015) Macroeconomic consequences of terrorist attacks: estimation for the analysis of policies and rules. In: Mansfield C, Smith VK (eds) Benefit transfer for the analysis of DHS policies and rules. Edward Elgar, Cheltenham

Rose A, Huyck C (2016) Improving catastrophe modeling for business interruption insurance needs. Risk Anal

Rose A, Krausmann E (2013) An economic framework for the development of a resilience index for business recovery. Int J Disaster Risk Reduct 5:73–83

Rose A, Liao S (2005) Modeling resilience to disasters: computable general equilibrium analysis of a water service disruption. J Reg Sci 45(1):75–112

Rose A, Lim D (2002) Business interruption losses from natural hazards: conceptual and methodology issues in the case of the Northridge earthquake. Environ Hazards Hum Soc Dimens 4:1–14

Rose A, Wei D (2013) Estimating the economic consequences of a port shutdown: the special role of resilience. Econ Syst Res 25(2):212–232

Rose A, Oladosu G, Liao S (2007) Business interruption impacts of a terrorist attack on the electric power system of Los Angeles: customer resilience to a total blackout. Risk Anal 27(3):513–531

Rose A, Oladosu G, Lee B, Beeler-Asay G (2009) The economic impacts of the 2001 terrorist attacks on the World Trade Center: a computable general equilibrium analysis. Peace Econ Peace Sci Public Policy 15(2):4

Rose A, Liao S, Bonneau A (2011a) Regional economic impacts of a Verdugo Earthquake disruption of Los Angeles water supplies: a computable general equilibrium analysis. Earthq Spectra 27(3):881–906

Rose A, Wei D, Wein A (2011b) Economic impacts of the ShakeOut Scenario. Earthq Spectra 27(2):539–557

Rose A, Sue Wing I, Wei D, Wein A (2016) Economic impacts of a California tsunami. Nat Hazards Rev 17(2):04016002

Rose A, Prager F, Chen Z, Chatterjee S, Wei D, Heatwole N, Warren E (2017) Economic consequence analysis tool (E-CAT). Springer, Tokyo. In press

Shi P, Jaeger C, Ye Q (2013) Integrated risk governance-science plan and case studies of large-scale disasters. Beijing Normal University Press/Springer, Heidelberg/Berlin

Tierney K (2014) The social roots of risk: producing disasters, promoting resilience. Stanford University Press, Stanford

Valle L, Campanella T (2005) The resilient city: how modern cities recover from disaster. Oxford University Press, New York

Contents

About the Author

Dr. Adam Rose is a research professor at the University of Southern California Sol Price School of Public Policy, and a faculty affiliate of the USC's Center for Risk and Economic Analysis of Terrorism Events (CREATE). He received his PhD in economics from Cornell University. Professor Rose's primary research interest is the economics of disasters. He has spearheaded the development of CREATE's comprehensive economic consequence analysis framework and contributed pioneering research on resilience at the level of the individual business, industry and macro economy. He has also completed dozens of case studies on disaster consequences, resilience, and recovery. His recent research has been funded by the National Science Foundation (NSF), World Bank, United Nations Development Programme, and Federal Emergency Management Agency (FEMA), as well as several other Department of Homeland Security (DHS) offices and components. Professor Rose is the author of several books and 250 professional papers, and has served on the editorial boards of a dozen journals in the disasters, environmental, and energy fields. He is the recipient of several awards including the International Society for Integrated Disaster Risk Management (IDRiM) Outstanding Research Award.

Chapter 1
Introduction

Human development throughout the world confronts many uncertainties in everyday life. It also faces serious challenges from infrequent, extreme events, both natural and man-made (UNDP 2012). Those living in developing countries are relatively less able to prevent these crises, less able to withstand them, and less able to rebound. These groups have relatively fewer resources and lower levels of resilience capacities. They are therefore also less able to manage their remaining scarce resources effectively during recovery and less able to rebuild rapidly if at all. The bottom income strata are especially vulnerable, as they tend to live disproportionately in low-lying areas subject to riverine or coastal flooding, along mountain slopes prone to landslides, in dilapidated housing in earthquake fault zones, and near industrial sites that generate toxic pollutants. Many developing countries also have unstable governments that make some form of persistent armed conflict relatively more prevalent.

Crises interrupt the course of human development and some may even threaten survival. Resilience is a broad term to cover ways individuals, communities, countries and regions respond to these threats. For now, we offer the following broad definition by Wilbanks (2009):

> A resilient community anticipates problems, opportunities, and potential for surprises, reduces vulnerabilities relative to development paths, social and economic conditions, and sensitivities to possible threats; responds effectively, fairly and legitimately in the event of an emergency; and recovers rapidly, better, safer, and fairer.

The major elements of this concept are captured more simply in the National Research Council (2012) definition:

> Resilience is the ability to prepare and plan for, absorb, recover from or more successfully adapt to actual or potential adverse events.

The purpose of this volume is to define, measure, and apply the concept of economic resilience from societal, environmental, and personal security perspectives. We explore major dimensions of economic resilience and their implications for

A. Rose, *Defining and Measuring Economic Resilience from a Societal, Environmental and Security Perspective*, Integrated Disaster Risk Management,
DOI 10.1007/978-981-10-1533-5_1

human development. We emphasize resilience as a coping mechanism for dealing with short-term crises, such as natural disasters and acts of terrorism. An example would be evacuation of a geographic area due to riverine flooding. In this example, evacuation can be contrasted with migration, which is a form of adaptation to long-run, or chronic, problems of climate change due to coastal erosion. A special aspect of the volume is to understand how lessons learned in the short-run out of necessity and through the application of human ingenuity, can be incorporated into long-run sustainability practices. In part, this stems from viewing resilience as a process, and one that enhances individual and societal competencies.

1.1 Human Development and Resilience

Resilience plays a major role in *human development*. As originally set forth in the 1990 UNDP Human Development Report (HDR), development is essentially a process that enlarges the range of choices for people to achieve their full potential UNDP, 1990. The 1990 HDR proposed a Human Development Index (HDI) with three pillars: life expectancy, literacy, and command over resources (including shelter and infrastructure). This index, though limited in scope and subject to the same shortcomings as most indices, offered excellent insights in its application to a broad range of countries. It essentially provides a benchmark of the status of human development in a given country and a way to gauge future progress.

The 1990 HDR emphasized that human development was "people-oriented." As was the case in Adam Smith's classic treatise that serves as the basis of modern economics, it viewed the wealth of a nation as inherently being its people. It emphasized the importance of public participation and how this leads to empowerment, which in turn facilitates people attaining and better utilizing their abilities (especially women and minorities, whose progress on these fronts has historically been stunted). Also important was the role of freedom for several reasons, but participation and removal of obstacles to using abilities and resources to promote development are seen as especially worthwhile. For example, in comparing HDIs across countries, the more democratic ones had higher scores. The report focused on distributional issues and equity of opportunities, processes, and outcomes, again as an avenue for promoting human development. It also had a strong sustainability theme, including a long-run view of the development process, emphasizing that this perspective is necessary to avoid actions taken today undercutting the well-being of future generations. It noted that poverty was a major threat to the environment and hence to sustainability principles.

The 2014 HDR (UNDP 2014) report modifies the three pillars of human development in relation to resilience with respect to: reductions in vulnerabilities and deepening of progress, linking vulnerability to threats and materialization of depravation of capacities, and policy formation for the public provision of goods and services. It stresses that uncertainty, especially pertinent to short-run shocks that typically arise without warning, has key implications at all levels of governance. And furthermore, governance issues are especially critical in reducing conflict.

While much of the 2014 HDR continues to emphasize the long-run context and to focus on structural and systemic resilience issues, this chapter focuses on resilience in response to shocks, mainly short-term, such as floods, earthquakes, terrorist attacks, and nuclear power accidents, but it does also addresses slow-onset, long-term threats such as sea-level rise and desertification. It also discusses the bridging of the short-run and long-run. Most fundamentally, societies that do not respond well to short-run shocks are not likely to be sustainable. A key is translating lessons learned about successful responses to short-run crises into long-run capabilities, behavior, and policies.

Combining the resilience definition in the Introduction of this volume and the attributes just discussed, and insights presented in various HDR reports, we enumerate several specific ways that resilience relates to human development in the context of disasters:

- Resilience to disasters is a key to increasing life expectancy.
- Literacy should be more broadly defined to include knowledge of disaster threats, vulnerabilities and coping mechanisms.
- Disasters reduce resource bases and make the management of remaining resources all the more critical.
- Many facets of human security, such as freedom from want and fear and the importance of living in dignity, are all the more challenged in a disaster context.
- The vicious circle of poverty and environmental degradation are exacerbated by disasters.
- Human security declines leading to short-run deprivation are likely to have even more dramatic long-run consequences.
- Development involves "building," whether physical structures or human capacity, and incorporating resilience at the outset is less costly than in the long run than retrofitting or not incorporating it at all.
- Public participation empowers people to contribute and also to acknowledge their responsibilities.
- Women represent an underutilized pool of talent in coping with disasters.
- Well-designed public policy is a key to improving resilience.
- People temporarily or permanently displaced by disasters are especially vulnerable.
- Development involves extensive institution building, and so does resilience.
- Resilience poses many challenges, as does human development, but also greater opportunities for cooperation in crises, where lasting effects on relations between countries can be improved.
- Sharing of resilience experiences is as valuable as sharing human development experiences.
- Disasters tear the social fabric of society, so key to human development.

- Diversification is a good development strategy, and is also a good strategy for reducing disaster vulnerability.
- Development requires the maturing and orderly functioning of markets, which can serve as an excellent source of resilience by providing signals on increased scarcity value of goods and services.
- Many resilience strategies are consistent with development strategies for the wise utilization of resources.
- Disasters make individuals more susceptible to social and political chaos in general, and crime and terrorism in particular.
- Resilience indicators have all the challenges of the human development index in general.

Overall, resilience is viewed as a way of deepening and sustaining human progress. It is also seen as a way to make the best of tragedies by turning them into opportunities.

1.2 Overview

This chapter has summarized the relationship between resilience and human development in general. Chapter 2 presents an economic framework for analysis, including principles that are important for understanding the role of resilience to individual decision-makers in the economy as a whole. Chapter 3 presents definitions of resilience from several major disciplines including: ecology, engineering, organizational behavior, psychology, sociology, planning, and economics. We cull out major attributes of resilience in these definitions and identify differences, but find that they are far outnumbered by the commonalities. Chapter 4 presents definitions of various types of economic resilience and their implications, and in Chap. 5 we explore their broader dimensions, and examine the relationship between resilience and several other key concepts such as vulnerability, adaptation, and sustainability. In Chap. 6, we discuss the measurement of economic resilience in terms of temporal, spatial, and scale dimensions. This involves examining the time-path of resilience and relating it to the recovery process. We discuss spatial variability in general, as well as the displacement of people within and across countries. In Chap. 7 we summarize empirical findings on measuring resilience. This includes evaluating progress on the formulation of resilience indices. Chapter 8 presents a risk-management framework, including aspects of cost-effectiveness and cost-benefit analysis. In Chap. 9 we explore co-benefits of disaster risk management in general and the important role of resilience. We conclude with a discussion of how short-run resilience actions can be transformed into long-run sustainability practices that help to avoid backsliding in our progress on human development.

References

National Research Council (2012) Disaster resilience: a national imperative. National Academy Press, Washington, DC

United Nations Development Programme (UNDP) (1990) Human development report 1990: concept and measurements of human development. United Nations, New York

United Nations Development Programme (UNDP) (2012) Human development report 2012: putting resilience at the heart of development: investing in prevention and resilient recovery. United Nations, New York

United Nations Development Programme (UNDP) (2014) Human development report 2014: sustaining human progress: reducing vulnerabilities and building resilience. United Nations, New York

Wilbanks T (2009) How geographic scale matters in seeking community resilience. CARRI Research Paper Number 7. Community and Resilience Institute, ORNL

Chapter 2
Economic Framework

The quantification of economic losses from natural and man-made hazards is necessary to gauge individual and community vulnerability, evaluate the worthiness of mitigation and resilience, determine the appropriate level of disaster assistance, improve recovery decisions, and inform insurers of their potential liability. Several major studies setting forth principles of hazard loss estimation have been undertaken in recent years, including National Research Council (1999), Heinz Center (2000), MMC (2005), and Rose (2004, 2009b).

The purpose of this chapter is to identify major issues surrounding conceptual and empirical aspects of disaster hazard loss estimation, more recently termed economic consequence analysis (ECA) (Rose 2015). This includes clarifying basic economic principles of loss estimation, such as the need to consider both property damage and business interruption, the distinction between direct and indirect losses, and real resource costs and transfers. It emphasizes the importance of the spatial and temporal context in which a natural or man-made disaster takes place, and the fact that hazard losses are highly variable because of business/consumer resilience and public policy.

2.1 Basic Principles

2.1.1 Welfare Economics

Welfare economics, the scientific basis for economic policy-making (see, e.g., Boardman et al. 2010), provides a starting point for an analysis of economic losses from natural and man-made hazards. A major point is that cost should be measured in terms of the value of resources used (or destroyed) and at prices that represent their efficient allocation, and not necessarily at market prices, which often do not account for inefficiencies, may not even exist in cases such as environmental

A. Rose, *Defining and Measuring Economic Resilience from a Societal, Environmental and Security Perspective*, Integrated Disaster Risk Management,
DOI 10.1007/978-981-10-1533-5_2

resources, or, more broadly, where massive destruction has caused turmoil in the market institution. This provides a guide for covering all resources, including non-market ones, and avoiding double-counting.

Business interruption losses represent a proxy for the ideal resource valuation because of the difficulty of measuring the latter. Hence, businesses, insurers, and governments typically make decisions on the basis of such metrics as lost sales revenue or profits.

Economists distinguish between gross output, the total value of production or sales, including the production of intermediate goods (industrial goods used to produce other goods), and net output, the value of final products. On the income side, net output is equivalent to the return to primary factors of production (labor, capital, natural resources, in the form of wages, profits and royalties). This is sometimes confusing because the major macroeconomic indicator, gross national product (GNP), is really a net measure, except that it includes depreciation. When depreciation is subtracted, the quantity is referred to as net national product. Business interruption losses are in gross terms if measured by lost production or sales, and they are in net terms if measured by lost wages, profits, and royalties.

Measurement is further complicated when what economists call "welfare" (well-being) metrics are calculated, typically using the concepts of producer and consumer surplus (see, e.g., Zerbe and Dively 2004). The former is equivalent to economic profits, or net returns of business (including deducting a market rate of return on investment and deducting depreciation). The latter includes consumer satisfaction from goods and services in excess of their market price, a concept very difficult to measure. It is no wonder that concepts like sales revenue are used as a proxy in everyday decision-making.[1]

2.1.2 Stocks Versus Flows

One of the fundamental distinctions recognized in economics is between *stocks* and *flows*. Stocks refer to a quantity at a single point in time, whereas flows refer to the services or outputs of stocks over time. Property damage represents a decline in stock value and usually leads to a decrease in service flows. Business interruption (BI) losses are a flow measure, but can emanate in part from a company's own property damage.

Property damage estimates have dominated loss reporting until recently, but flow measures are important in their own right. First, in recent major disasters, such as the 9/11 World Trade Center Attacks and Hurricane Katrina, BI losses have far exceeded property damage.

[1] It should be noted that the use of GDP underestimates the pure Welfare impact. It only values goods at their price, which, except for the marginal consumer is lower than the willingness to pay of all other consumers. Similarly, the sales price for the marginal producer may be equal to marginal cost, but it is higher than the marginal cost for all other producers.

Second, direct BI losses can take place even in the absence of property damage, and hence represent broader coverage of the scope of losses. For example, a factory may be unscathed by an earthquake, but may be forced to shut down if its electricity supply is cut off due to earthquake-induced damage to power stations, substations, transmission lines, or distribution lines.[2]

A third reason flow measures are useful is that they are more consistent with indices of individual wellbeing, such as consumer satisfaction and business profits, or with aggregate measures, such as gross national (or regional) product. In this regard, property damage measures can exaggerate losses because only a portion of the property value translates into service flows in any 1 year. Additional reasons flow measures are superior is that they have a time dimension and are more readily linked to the majority of indirect effects (see below).

The major reason flow measures are superior to stock measures is that the former include a time dimension. Stock measures pertain simply to the value of an asset at a single point in time. The typical measure of damage (purchase or replacement cost) is thus invariant to how long the asset is out of service. For example, if the roof of a factory is blown off by a hurricane, there is a tendency to specify the loss in fixed terms, irrespective of whether production is shut down for a week or a year awaiting repairs. This makes all the difference with respect to BI.

Attention to flow losses represents a major shift in the focus of hazard loss estimation—that losses are not a definite or set amount but are highly variable depending on the length of the "economic disruption," typically synonymous with the recovery plus reconstruction periods. This also brings home the point that disaster losses are not simply determined by the strength of the stimulus (coupled with initial exposure and modified by mitigation that reduces vulnerability), but also highly dependent on human ingenuity, will, and resources following the shock. Caution should be exercised, however, before rushing toward minimizing losses without consideration of the increased recovery costs incurred. The broader objective is to minimize the joint cost of impacts and recovery/reconstruction. Fortunately, a set of costless, or near costless, tactics to greatly reduce BI losses during the recovery period exist in the form of resilience (see, e.g., Rose 2004, 2009). These include both market (private sector) and non-market (public policy responses) to be discussed further below.

---

[2] The value of an asset is the discounted flow of net future returns from its operation. Hence, for ordinary property damage the stock and flow measures represent the same things, and, at first pass, including both would involve double-counting. The situation is, however, complicated in the case of natural hazards. This is a controversial subject. I am in agreement with analysts who suggest it is appropriate to include both the stock and flow measures in the case of damaged property, but only where the latter is confined to the opportunity costs of delays in restoring production because of the repair and reconstruction process.

2.1.3 Double-Counting

In addition to some stock/flow overlaps, care should be taken to avoid other types of double-counting of hazard losses. Many goods and services have quite diverse attributes, and all of those damaged/interrupted should be counted (e.g., a hydroelectric dam provides electricity, recreational opportunities in the reservoir behind it, and flood control). It is important, however, to remember that some goods and services cannot yield all of these attributes to their maximum simultaneously, and that only one or the other, or some balance of the two, should only be counted (e.g., a river can provide services to swimmers or it can be a repository for waste but not both at the same time).

Double-counting can be avoided by not attributing losses to more than one entity in the case of private goods, as in the case of avoiding counting retail store sales as a loss to both the storeowner and its customers. Just as important, however, is the inclusion of all relevant losing entities or stakeholders. Caution must be exercised here because of the regional character of most hazards and the inclination just to consider those living within its boundaries. Tourism associated with natural environments is an excellent case in point. Loss of environmental value should not just be gauged by local residents and also not by current users but by all potential users in terms of a concept known as option demand (Freeman et al. 2014).

A closely related consideration pertains to the distinction between costs and transfers. If the expenditures needed to repair flood damage to a bridge are $10 million, and 5 % of the expenditures were various types of taxes (sales, import tariffs, property, etc.), taxes do not reflect the use of resources and are not real costs to society. In general, such taxes are important to individual households or businesses, but simply represent a shifting of dollars from one entity to another. The complication that arises here, however, pertains to the spatial delineation of the affected group. Local property or sales taxes within a region are transfers, but payments of federal income tax do represent an outflow and can be legitimately included in the regional cost estimates. Of course, there is the danger of being too provincial in such assessments.[3]

2.1.4 Direct Versus Higher-Order Effects

The distinction between direct and indirect effects has been the subject of great confusion in hazard loss estimation from the outset. For example, the characterization that direct loss pertains to property damage and indirect loss pertains to business interruption (see, e.g., ATC 1991; Heinz Center 2000) is not helpful because

---

[3] Some taxes, such as property taxes, do reflect an indirect payment for services, such as water and sewer, but tariffs and sales taxes do not. Property taxes would only be included in the resource cost tabulation if the water and sewer services were actually used in the construction of the hydroelectric dam and then only at a level commensurate with the service costs.

both have direct and indirect components.[4] While total business interruption losses are the bottom line, distinguishing components helps ensure everything is counted and provides more precise information for decision-making (e.g., as illustrated below, direct effects usually pertain to private concerns of individual businesses, while indirect effects raise additional public policy issues).

Direct flow losses pertain to production in businesses damaged by the hazard itself, or what the NRC (1999, p. 15) study refers to as the "consequences" of physical destruction, though without distinguishing direct vs. indirect components as does Mileti (1999; p. 98). They have also come to include lost production stemming from direct loss of public utility and infrastructure services (Rose et al. 2011). For example, earthquake-induced disruptions of water supplies may force the closing of a high-rise office building for fire safety reasons (fire engine hoses can only reach the first several floors, and the remainder of fire control is dependent on internal sprinkling systems). A factory may have to shut down because the bridge that its suppliers and employers use to reach it is damaged. Again, the office building and factory may not suffer any direct physical damage.

The extent of BI does not stop here, but sets off a chain reaction. A factory shutdown will reduce supplies to its customers, who may be forced to curtail their production for lack of critical inputs. In turn, their customers may be forced to do the same, as will the customers of these customers, and so on. These types of effects are called downstream, forward, or supply-side linkages. A set of counterparts refers to upstream, backward linkage, or demand-side indirect effects. The factory shutdown will also reduce orders for its inputs. Its suppliers will then have to reduce their production and hence cancel orders for their inputs. The suppliers of the suppliers will follow suit, and so forth. The sum total of all of these indirect effects is a multiple of the direct effects; hence, the concept of a "multiplier" is often applied to their estimation (Rose and Miernyk 1989; FEMA 2014).[5] The state of the art modeling approach, computable general equilibrium (CGE) analysis, has gained prominence in ECA (see, e.g., Rose 2005, 2015. It is able to estimate a broader range of "higher-order" impacts, typically referred to as "general equilibrium" effects, which, rather than being confined to economic interdependence (based solely on

[4] Indirect effects can also be associated with stock losses or property damage (e.g., earthquakes causing damage from fires, hazardous materials leakages, and buildings made more vulnerable to subsequent weather damage). However, except in extreme cases, such as the 2011 Japanese earthquake and tsunami followed by the Fukushima nuclear reactor accident, these indirect stock effects are likely to be relatively small when compared with the flow-induced indirect losses

[5] Some further clarification is in order. First, the current line of demarcation between direct and indirect effects is somewhat arbitrary, specifically, the convention of counting business losses due to cut-off from utility lifelines as direct effects. There is equal justification for considering these to be first-round indirect effects. The advantage to including these as direct losses is that it emphasizes the key role of utilities and infrastructure in the economy, and emphasizes their prominent role in contributing to losses. Also, it helps ensure that these effects will be taken into account, because most analysts are not able to or do not bother to consider what are termed "indirect" effects.

quantities of inputs and outputs), also capture responses to price changes in factor and product markets (Dixon and Rimmer 2002; Rose et al. 2017).

Many analysts are hesitant to measure higher-order losses for various reasons. First, they cannot be as readily verified as direct losses. Second, modeling them requires utilizing simple economic models carefully, or, more recently, utilizing quite sophisticated economic models. Third, the size of higher-order effects can be quite variable depending on the resiliency of the economy and the pace and pattern of recovery (see, e.g., Rose et al. 1997, as well as the discussions and illustrations below). Fourth is the danger of manipulating these effects for political purposes (e.g., it is not unusual in the context of economic development for promoters to inflate multipliers). However, none of these reasons undercut the importance of higher-order effects, especially if one considers that their likely size is often greater than direct effects (see, e.g., Cochrane 1997; Webb et al. 2000; Bram et al. 2002).

2.2 Non-market Effects

Hazard researchers are becoming increasingly aware of the ever-broader scope of disaster losses. Heinz (2000) does an excellent job of enumerating their extent, including categories of Social, Health and Safety, and Eco-System costs. Most of the losses in the latter category, as well as a significant portion of losses to one of the other two categories identified in the Heinz Report—the Built Environment—are characterized by economists as "non-market." This means they are not bought or sold and hence do not readily have a price tag. However, just because something does not have a price does not mean it does not have value; it simply means a "market failure" has occurred. In this case, a market will fail to perform it major function, because the absence of prices will cause resources to be misallocated.

The major area of attention to non-market aspects of natural hazards to date has been on one part of the built environment—public infrastructure, such as highways/bridges and utility lifelines (electricity, gas, and water). Non-market effects arise here primarily because the former category is typically publicly (rather than privately) owned, and hence services are typically provided without exacting a direct payment, and/or because both categories have features of decreasing cost activities (natural monopolies), and appropriate pricing is made difficult (see also Howe and Cochrane 1993).[6]

[6] Both eco-system losses and public infrastructure losses arise in the context of what economists call "public goods," which have the characteristics that two or more people can utilize the services of the good simultaneously without detracting completely from one another, and from which people cannot be excluded because it is technologically impossible, socially unacceptable, or economically impractical. Major examples of public goods are national defense, television broadcasting signals, national parks, and environmental resources in general. This is in contrast to more typical "private goods," which are utilized by one person at a time and for which a price can readily be extracted (e.g., clothing, restaurant meals, etc.). Not all public goods are provided by government; some are provided by the private sector under the right circumstances, and most

The various flow impacts of natural hazards on the public sector built environment have been termed "infrastructure user costs" (see Rose et al. 1998). For the case of a highway washed away by a flood, there is no direct production loss measure, e.g., no lost public highway "sales," except in the case of toll roads, where the toll is not necessarily an accurate measure of lost value in any case. Direct losses would, according to the convention noted earlier, best be represented by lost revenue of businesses that are required to shut down because their employees could not get to work, inputs could not be accessed, or outputs could not be delivered.

Several other non-market direct impacts take place, however, as do conventional market and unconventional non-market higher-order impacts. Commuters are adversely impacted by transportation outages through loss of time due to congestion (even the subsequently decreased leisure time has a value); however, there are no multiplier effects associated with this activity. On the other hand, the loss of productivity to producers or transportation companies results in cost increases that have price multiplier effects first (a form of "cost-push" inflation) and output multiplier effects subsequently. Consumers may also curtail their shopping trips due to bridge or highway outages. These decreases in direct consumption also generate higher-order effects (see, e.g., Gordon et al. 1998).

For the case of utility lifelines, direct and indirect production losses are likely to be the major loss category. Production losses stem from downtime or decline in product quality and will spawn multiplier effects, as in the transportation example. Decreases in household activity (reduced showers, reading time, cooking) are not part of economic indices, but they should be considered in broader measures of well-being, though multiplier effects are not applicable (Rose and Oladosu 2008).[7] The consumer side is important but lifeline disruptions will have little effect on shopping over and above that attributable to business operation itself. For example, if a power outage causing the closure of a department store were listed as a direct output (sales) loss for the producer, it would be double-counting if included as a consumption loss as well.

The largest potential area of non-market losses pertains to the natural environment, ranging from conventionally marketed economic activity, such as agriculture

environmental goods are provided by nature. There is considerable momentum to reduce the number of goods and services provided by government, even for what were previously thought to be public goods. This involves enhancing the "excludability" characteristics so that a user fee can be charged. This is not necessarily simple since efficient pricing would actually require that different users be assessed different charges, according to their marginal willingness to pay. Another complication is that some goods have different values and different degrees of "publicness" at different times (a classic example is a road, which can accommodate traffic at zero cost during normal hours, but that is subject to congestion, which imposes costs on all users during peak hours). Several remedies to this situation have been proposed, as well as for the more complicated situation where periods of congestion (and hence increasing costs) exist. All of these remedies require careful scrutiny to make sure that the price charged represents accurate valuation of the resources used.

[7] Property damage to residential structures also has a flow counterpart, termed the "imputed rental value of owner-occupied dwellings." This non-market cost might be measured as well; it has no higher-order effects, except those associated with payments for temporary shelter.

and forestry, but extending to damages to the environment in general, even including "option value" (in part, the value one places on potential access to the resource in the future). An extensive literature on non-market valuation exists (see, e.g., Freeman et al. 2014) but was largely unnoticed by hazard researchers, though it is a major focus of the closely related area of research on damages from climate change (see, e.g., IPCC 2014). Note that while climate change is usually characterized by long-term warming, it also gives rise to short-term climate variability, which many scientists have concluded manifests itself in increasing frequency and magnitude of hurricanes and other types of severe storms that can lead to direct and indirect losses through water or wind damage.

2.3 Distributional Considerations

Often neglected in hazard loss estimation and ECA is the distribution of costs and benefits. These considerations relate to how impacts are spread across regions, sectors and socioeconomic groups. Most of loss estimates to date in this area have disaggregated their results by economic sector, fewer by region, and even fewer by income bracket or race/ethnicity.

Distributional considerations are important for at least three reasons. First, numerous studies have determined that the least well-off and minority groups are those most vulnerable to disasters; moreover, their condition is exacerbated by these events (Mileti 1999). Thus, disasters are a great concern from an equity, or justice, standpoint. Second, lagging socioeconomic groups or lagging regions have been found to represent a drag on economic growth and development. Third, identifying the impacts on various stakeholders provides insight into the motivations of government decision-makers and the likelihood of support or lack of support for disaster risk management policies. Distributional information can better inform stakeholders and thus enhance the public participation process, as well as serving as a predictive tool for the decisions the process is likely to yield. Used appropriately, distributional information can fill in many needed informational gaps and help lead to a more enlightened citizenry, and hence decisions more attuned to the needs of the public (Rose et al. 1988).

Distributional impacts are likely to be more controversial than aggregate ones but no less important. For example, achieving accuracy is more difficult for subsets of a region. Also, there is likely to be a mismatch between those who may have to incur the costs of mitigation or post-disaster recovery and those who benefit from their implementation. Still, accurate distributional estimates are a useful supplement to the aggregate numbers used in most benefit-cost analyses (BCA). Ordinary BCA implicitly justifies decisions on the basis of how the community is impacted as a whole. It works well in the context of a single, custodial decision-maker (increasingly less the case these days), or, in the case of public participation if people are entirely altruistic (also unlikely). Distributional information, on the other hand, can help affected parties to see what stake they have in dealing with natural hazards. At the very least, this will help make potential impacts more poignant and generate greater interest in the issue.

Distributional loss estimation also addresses the increasingly prominent issue of "environmental justice," which has typically been applied to evaluating differential environmental impacts of public policy across racial/ethnic groups (Schlosberg 2007). This topic is important for reasons of fairness, but also for pragmatic reasons relating to lawsuits brought by minority group members when they have felt an unequal burden of environmental damage and can readily be extended to natural hazard damage, or felt they were incurring a disproportionate percentage of the cost of mitigation or remediation.

The distribution of hazard impacts is often omitted because of lack of models or data. However, the models discussed below are well-suited to performing distributional analysis of natural hazards, and have been applied extensively to related contexts of climate change policy (see, e.g., Kverndokk and Rose 2008; Rose et al. 2012). They disaggregate the economy into sectors, providing insight to the inherent unevenness of direct and higher-order impacts across industries and between industries, households, government, and other institutions. Many of the models allow for further analysis of socioeconomic or institutional accounts by disaggregating income, consumption, and trade flows (Batey and Rose 1990; Hanson and Rose 1997; IMPLAN 2016).[8] This modeling is reasonably straightforward, including calculation of short-cut distributional multipliers, e.g., how a direct change in income to one socioeconomic group affects all others directly and indirectly (see, e.g., Okuyama et al. 1999). The major limitation is data, especially mapping of income flows from sectors to socioeconomic groups. Still, some useful data reduction and adaptation techniques exist here as well (see Rose et al. 1988; Li et al. 1999), so that this area of application is considered to be reasonably accurate, though not as much as aggregate impact estimation.

References

Applied Technology Council (1991) ATC-25: seismic vulnerability and impact of disruption on lifelines in the conterminous United States. Federal Emergency Management Agency, Applied Technology Council, Redwood City

Batey P, Rose A (1990) Extended input-output models: progress and potential. Int Reg Sci Rev 13:27–49

Boardman A et al (2010) Cost-benefit analysis: concepts and practice, 4th edn. Prentice Hall, Upper Saddle River

Bram J, Orr J, Rappaport C (2002) The impact of the world trade center attack on New York City: where do we stand? Federal Reserve Bank of New York, New York

---

[8]The number of income brackets is limited by the availability of data but typically involves as many as ten separate classes. Extensive disaggregations of occupational groups are possible because of the longstanding work of the U.S. Bureau of Labor Statistics. Disaggregations according to racial/ethnic groups are more difficult, but a good deal of data is generally available from the U.S. Bureau of Census.

Cochrane H (1997) Forecasting the economic impact of a mid-west earthquake. In: Jones B (ed) Economic consequences of earthquakes: preparing for the unexpected. MCEER, Buffalo
Dixon P, Rimmer M (2002) Dynamic general equilibrium modelling for forecasting and policy: a practical guide and documentation of MONASH. North-Holland, Amsterdam
Federal Emergency Management Agency (FEMA) (2014) Multi-hazard loss estimation methodology (HAZUS®MH MR4). Federal Emergency Management Agency, Washington, DC
Freeman A, Herriges J, Kling K (2014) The measurement of environmental and resource values: theory and methods. Resources for the Future, Washington, DC
Gordon P, Richardson H, Davis B (1998) Transport-related impacts of the Northridge earthquake. J Transp Stat 1:22–36
Hanson K, Rose A (1997) Factor productivity and income inequality: a general equilibrium analysis. Appl Econ 29:1061–1171
Heinz Center for Science, Economics and the Environment (2000) The hidden costs of coastal hazards: implications for risk assessment and mitigation. Island Press, Washington, DC
Howe C, Cochrane H (1993) Guidelines for the uniform definition, identification and measurement of economic damages from natural hazard events. Program on Environment and Behavior Special Publication No. 28. Institute of Behavioral Science, University of Colorado, Boulder
Impact Analysis for Planning (IMPLAN) (2016) Huntersville, NC. http://implan.com/
Intergovernmental Panel on Climate Change (IPCC) (2014) Climate change 2014: synthesis report. Cambridge University Press, New York
Kverndokk S, Rose A (2008) Equity and justice in global warming policy. Int Rev Environ Resour Econ 2(2):135–176
Li PC, Rose A, Eduardo B (1999) Construction of an input-output income distribution matrix for the U.S. In: Hewings GJD et al (eds) Understanding and interpreting economic structure. Springer, Heidelberg
Mileti D (1999) Disasters by design: a reassessment of natural hazards in the United States. Joseph Henry Press, Washington, DC
Multihazard Mitigation Council (MMC) (2005) Natural hazard mitigation saves: an independent study to assess the future savings from mitigation activities. Report to U.S. Congress on behalf of the National Institute of Building Sciences, Washington, DC.
National Research Council (1999) The impacts of natural disasters: a framework for loss estimation. National Academy of Sciences Press, Washington, DC
Okuyama Y, Hewings GJD, Kim T, Boyce D, Ham H, Sohn J (1999) Economic impacts of an earthquake in the New Madrid seismic zone: a multiregional analysis. In: Elliott W, McDonough P (eds) Optimizing post-earthquake lifeline system reliability. American Society of Civil Engineers, Reston
Rose A (2004) Economic principles, issues, and research priorities in natural hazard loss estimation. In: Okuyama Y, Chang S (eds) Modeling the spatial economic impacts of natural hazards. Springer, Heidelberg
Rose A (2005) Analyzing terrorist threats to the economy: a computable general equilibrium approach. In: Richardson H, Gordon P, Moore J (eds) Economic impacts of terrorist attacks. Edward Elgar Publishing Co., Cheltenham
Rose A (2009) A framework for analyzing and estimating the total economic impacts of a terrorist attack and natural disaster. J Homeland Secur Emerg Manage 6(1):Article 6
Rose A (2015) Macroeconomic consequences of terrorist attacks: estimation for the analysis of policies and rules. In: Mansfield C, Smith VK (eds) Benefit transfer for the analysis of DHS policies and rules. Edward Elgar, Cheltenham
Rose A, Miernyk W (1989) Input-output analysis: the first fifty years. Econ Syst Res 1:229–271
Rose A, Oladosu G (2008) Regional economic impacts of natural and man-made hazards disrupting utility lifeline services to households. In: Richardson H, Gordon P, Moore J (eds) Economic impacts of hurricane Katrina. Edward Elgar, Cheltenham
Rose A, Chang SE, Shinozuka M (1998) Direct and indirect infrastructure user costs of natural hazards. In: Proceedings of the structural engineers world congress. Elsevier, New York

Rose A, Liao S, Bonneau A (2011) Regional economic impacts of a Verdugo earthquake disruption of Los Angeles water supplies: a computable general equilibrium analysis. Earthq Spectra 27(3):881–906

Rose A, Stevens B, Davis G (1988) National resource policy and income distribution. Johns Hopkins University Press, Baltimore

Rose A, Wei D, Prager F (2012) Distributional impacts of greenhouse gas emissions trading: alternative allocation and recycling strategies in California. Contemp Econ Policy 30(4):603–617

Rose A, Prager F, Chen Z, Chatterjee S (2017) Economic consequence analysis tool (E-CAT), vol 2, Integrated disaster risk management. Springer, Singapore, forthcoming

Rose A, Benavides J, Chang SE, Szczesniak P, Lim D (1997) The regional economic impact of an earthquake: direct and indirect effects of electricity lifeline disruptions. J Reg Sci 37:437–458

Schlosberg D (2007) Defining environmental justice: theories, movements, and nature. Oxford University Press, New York/Oxford

Webb G, Tierney K, Dahlhamer J (2000) Business and disasters: empirical patterns and unanswered questions. Nat Hazards Rev 1:83–90

Zerbe R, Dively D (2004) Benefit-cost analysis: theory and practice, 2nd edn. HarperCollins, New York

Chapter 3
Defining Resilience Across Disciplines

The etymology of resilience is the Latin term *resilio*, meaning to rebound. Although published accounts of its use date back to ancient Rome in Cicero's *Orations* (Alexander 2013), and some physicists and psychologists in the early twentieth century (Manyena 2006), ecologists were the first to embrace and make extensive use of the general concept of resilience more than 30 years ago (see, e.g., Holling 1973). Since then, it has been adapted or re-invented for the case of short-term disasters (see, e.g., Tierney 1997; Bruneau et al. 2003; Rose 2004, 2007) and long-term phenomena, such as climate change (see, e.g., Dovers and Handmer 1992; IPCC 2007). The analysis of resilience can benefit from a comparison of its definitions in ecology, engineering, organizational behavior, planning, psychology, sociology and economics over the past 40 years. In the discussion below, we focus on points of agreement. This is the basis for establishing criteria for operational metrics that are consistent with fundamental principles, the needs of potential users, and the practical matters of data availability and computational manageability.

3.1 Ecological Origins

Ecologists have pioneered a useful, broad definition of resilience relating to the survival of complex systems. Holling's (1973; p. 17) definition is "the ability of systems to absorb changes … and still persist." He sometimes refers to it as "buffer capacity," and resilience is measured in this paradigm in relation to the size of the shock that is absorbed. Pimm (1991) is usually cited as the source of an alternative ecological emphasis in the definition of resilience in terms of the speed at which the system returns to equilibrium. In most disciplines, the term *resilience* is more in line with the buffer concept, as the ability to mute the influence of the external shock. It is not just the decrease in activity, but rather the decrease relative to the potential decrease from the external shock. Perrings (2001; p. 322) also defines resilience in

A. Rose, *Defining and Measuring Economic Resilience from a Societal, Environmental and Security Perspective*, Integrated Disaster Risk Management,
DOI 10.1007/978-981-10-1533-5_3

a relative manner: "As a first approximation, this may be measured by an index of the level of pollution or depletion relative to the assimilative or carrying capacity of the ecological system concerned." Subsequently, Perrings (p. 323) defines it in terms of the "gap between current and critical loads" to the ecosystem and even the ecological-economic system.

Here and below we distinguish the concept of resilience and related terms. For example, Holling (1973; p. 17) defines *stability* as "the ability of a system to return to equilibrium after a temporary disturbance." This definition is often put forth as the essence of resilience or at least a special dimension. However, it is clear that resilience and stability are distinct. As Handmer and Dovers (1996) point out, a stable system may not fluctuate significantly, but a resilient system may undergo significant fluctuation and return to a new (and possibly improved) equilibrium.

3.2 Individual Resilience

At the most fundamental level, resilience pertains to how individuals cope with crises, ranging from the death of a family bread winner by everyday occurrences to the less common but broader infrequent events affecting the entire community characterized as disasters. Likewise, children may have their education interrupted by a range of phenomena, including family pressures to work, as well as the destruction of their school by a hurricane. Resilience is applicable to the range of human experience coping with threats to human security, livelihoods and overall well-being. Resilience gets to the heart of the survival instinct that has been demonstrated consistently over eons. While mass panic is often attributed to such situations, research indicates that this is the exception rather than the rule (Mileti 1999). People everywhere are very adept at self-preservation and extending help not only to their families and neighbors, but also to complete strangers.

Another source of individual resilience stems from various economic roles, including producer, consumer, and provider of labor and capital services. Economic incentives help promote resilience, though this is affected by two key considerations. First, workers and managers only focus on the enterprise once they know their families are safe and receiving the proper care. Second, many disasters instill fear in people, which affects some of their behavior. This is all the more pronounced because of media attention and/or rumor, which contribute to the *social amplification of risk* in the short-run, and because of *stigma effects* for locations that have been hit by some disaster (such as those affected by accidental or intentional biological, chemical, or a radiological contamination) in the long-run. For example, the largest single factor contributing to the economic losses arising from a September 11, 2001, attack on the World Trade Center was the nearly 2-year reduction in air travel and related tourism (Rose et al. 2009). Another example is the study by Giesecke et al. (2012), which analyzed the effects of a simulated dirty bomb (radiological dispersion device) attack scenario on the financial district of Los Angeles in terms of potential demand for increased wages and rates of return, as well as shopper/

tourist discounts. The study found that these behavioral impacts were fifteen times the size of the ordinary economic losses typically measured. Recent research has focused on ways to reduce this fear through improved risk communications, which is yet another way of strengthening resilience (Rosoff et al. 2013)

Flynn (2008) has emphasized the key role of individuals in resilience, and sees resilience as empowering. It provides people the opportunity to reach their full potential in a crisis. It also provides cohesion to the community and nation. Flynn points out that "a terrorist chooses battlegrounds that are likely to be occupied by civilians, not soldiers" He notes the importance of resilience as a weapon against the spread of fear, one of terrorists' greatest objectives. One of the dividends of empowering individuals is that it releases an enormous amount of energy and skills to cope with disasters. Flynn also notes that empowering individuals lessens the paternalistic role of government in this disaster response. The actions of many governments that consistently bail out disaster victims, even if they have engaged in moral hazard (e.g., continuous rebuilding in flood plains), is a classic example (see, e.g., Mileti 1999).

Another strong role for the individual stems from a major theme of human development – public participation in decisions and processes. A related key theme is fairness, or equity, one version of which is the basis for promoting equality in both the participation and in the outcomes of resilient activities. It includes special consideration for the aged, the infirm, women, and racial/ethnic minorities.

Synergies and economies of scale and scope arise when individuals band together to address a crisis. Specialization, organizational memory, and official sanctioning are some of the many reasons for the formation of institutions in this area. Similar motivations, as well as motivations relating to social cohesion are the basis for community resilience at the neighborhood, town/city, province/state and national levels.

3.3 Community Resilience

Adger (2000) was one of the first to extend the ecological definition of resilience to human communities as a whole. He measured *social resilience* as related to social capital and in terms of economic factors (e.g., resource dependence), institutions (e.g., property rights), and demographics (e.g., migration). Norris et al. (2008) have approached the matter in a similar fashion for *community resilience*. They developed a framework for it that encompasses stress, adaptation, wellness and resource dynamics. They state that "community resilience is a process linking a network of adaptive capacities (resources with dynamic attributes) to adaptation after a disturbance or adversity." Adaptive capacities include economic development, social capital, information and communication, and community confidence. Community is defined in a broad sense to include both the built and natural environments and the economy in addition to the social structure. Still, the major focus is less on community organization than on preventing injury, both physical and mental.

Norris et al. (2008) defined population wellness as "a community-level outcome indicative of a successful adaptation, defined as high and non-disparate levels of mental and behavioral health, role functioning, and quality of life in constituent populations." They use "wellness" as an indicator of the success of adaptive resilience at the individual level. Psychological wellness is in turn defined according to four criteria: absence of psychopathology, healthy patterns of behavior, adequate role functioning, and high quality of life. They acknowledge that the community as a whole is greater than the sum of the parts. Community adaptation is then defined as population wellness, linked to a high prevalence of individual wellness in the community. They acknowledge, however, the "prevention paradox", where increases in individual wellness are marginal but lead to major improvements in community wellness, as all the individual advances are added up.

Norris et al. (2008) emphasized that resilience in general and resource mobilization in particular can be deteriorated by the presence of lingering threats. They cite the example of community's proximity to the Israel-Lebanon border and their exposure to political violence. This is consistent with Hobfoll's (1998) theory that stress is basically related to threats to resources, broadly defined. Compounding the problem is that the loss of resources in a disaster is shared by community members (Erickson 1976). Norris et al. (2008) emphasize that disasters affect entire communities, not just individuals.

In the Norris framework, resilience stems from a set of networked adaptive capacities. The adaptive aspect stems from a combination of resources themselves and community responses to crises. With regard to network resources, Norris et al. (2002) emphasize the importance of the resource base in economic development and note that socioeconomic status is a main indicator of vulnerability, especially in developing countries. Resilience is a function of the size and diversity of the resource base and also of resource equity. Social capital is a second important type of adaptive capital and stems from people using social networks primarily for personal gain. Support networks are especially important in disaster communication and recovery. For example, those linked into networks are more likely to evacuate and those connected to networks are more likely to engage in mutual support and cohesive behavior. Public participation is also a key feature of community resilience, as it is in other forms of resilience mentioned in this chapter.

3.4 Engineering

Bruneau et al. (2003) provide a comprehensive analysis of the many aspects of earthquake loss reduction, all under the heading of resilience. The authors apply the concept at four levels: technical, organizational, social, and economic. They contend that resilience has four dimensions: robustness (ability to withstand a shock), redundancy (e.g., parallel or back-up systems), resourcefulness (stabilizing measures), and rapidity (with respect to rebuilding and recovery). Bruneau et al. also stipulate that the resilience of a system has three aspects: reduced probability of failures, reduced consequences from failures, and reduced time to recovery. These pertain more to the general risk equation but have obvious overlaps with the four dimensions.[1]

A major criticism of the definition of Bruneau et al. (2003) is that they include all aspects of hazard loss reduction under the banner of resilience, including mitigation (see also Linkov et al. 2013). This is not surprising, as the greatest effectiveness of engineering is in protecting the built environment, as opposed to the individual, organizational, and community activities involved in post-disaster recovery. This is in contrast to the position of Klein et al. (2003) (and many others) to keep the definition of resilience from becoming too broad. They propose the concept of "adaptive capacity" as the more appropriate umbrella concept that covers many of the features identified by Bruneau et al. This is also more consistent with defining resilience as an outcome or system attribute rather than as a tactic like mitigation. Chang and Shinozuka (2004; p. 741) state that: "It is useful to view robustness and rapidity as the desired *ends* of resilience-enhancing measures. Redundancy and resourcefulness are some of the *means* to these ends."

It would appear that Bruneau et al., as well as non-engineers such as Mileti (1999), have envisioned a goal of a community that is able to take many steps to minimize its vulnerability to hazards. Resilience has become a convenient term to characterize all of these possibilities. However, this broad usage is inconsistent with the etymology of the term in general and its use in ecology, economics and other areas of research. Ideally, another term can be found to characterize this ideal community, so that the term "resilience" can be applied to the sub-set of characteristics to which it is best suited.

3.5 Organizational Behavior

Organizational (and the closely related area of institutional) behavior focuses on resilience as a process (Hill and Paton 2005). As such, it is a strategy in risk management under the sub-heading of crisis and continuity management. Paton and Johnston (2001) define resilience in this dimension as "a capacity of people and systems that facilitate organizational performance to maintain functional relationships in the presence of significant disturbances as a result of a capability to draw upon their resources and competencies to manage the demands, challenges and changes encountered." This viewpoint extends even more fundamentally to natural ecosystems, whereby The Resilience Alliance (2005) includes as one of its three dimensions of resilience "the degree to which the system is capable of reorganization." Adger et al. (2005) extend this to the social-ecological nexus.

Comfort (1994) confines resilience to actions and processes after the event occurs, or, to the *consequences* of failure. This also relates to process-oriented counterparts of the concept of dynamic resilience, where the focus is not on attaining a target level of output but rather a target level of "functioning." However, the trajec-

[1] The important role of human factors, especially in light of mounting technological complexity of engineered systems, should not be overlooked in this and other general frameworks (see, e.g., Meshkati and Yalda (2015).

tory of this functioning is clear from the major themes of non-linear and adaptive dynamics (Comfort 1999). It also leaves no doubt that the dynamic version of resilience (the rapidity to bounce back) is uniquely applicable to the post-disaster stages. Moreover, the recovery process this characterizes is another way of reducing the consequences of the hazard ensuing from structural or system damage. Manyena (2006) contends that resilience has evolved from an emphasis on outcomes to an emphasis on process in holistic terms (see also Pfefferbaum et al. 2005).

Klein et al. (2003) have taken this even further to suggest that resilience goes beyond the Holling definition to include the functioning and interaction of inter-linked systems (see also UN/ISDR 2002). However, this still does not go as far as suggesting that resilience includes all aspects of adaptation or mitigation.

In contrast to resilience activities emphasized in the economics literature, the focus of organizational theory is on "competencies and systems" (Hill and Paton 2005; see also an extension of this theme to the community as a set of networked adaptive capacities). The relationship between the two approaches can be viewed as follows: most standard treatments of resilience in engineering and economics identify a set of options and assume that managers can optimize among their choices (see, e.g., Rose and Liao 2005). Organizational analysis identifies vulnerabilities and limitations in managerial abilities and how they can be overcome through resilience. The economics approach to reconciling these two views would be to assume some form of "bounded rationality" (see, e.g., Gigerenzer and Selten 2002) and to view managerial resilience as an improvement over the basic outcome. Hill and Paton (2005) analyze several aspects of the theory and practice of business continuity management and how it relates to resilience. They emphasize that a major prerequisite of success in this area is the willingness of an organization to adapt to its new environment.

3.6 Planning

Sustainable communities and the supporting theme of smart growth emanate from the collaborative visions of ecologists, sociologists, geographers, economists, and planners. Thus far, the planners have been most prominent at practical approaches to the broader design, while the other disciplines have been more niche-oriented, including the nexus of ecological economics in reorienting individual business operations to principles of industrial metabolism (see, e.g., Ayres and Simonis 1989; Daly and Farley 2004).

The planning profession has as a goal the creation of hazard-resilient communities (Burby et al. 2000; Godschalk 2003), primarily through comprehensive land-use strategies known as "smart growth." This holistic approach is superior to the piecemeal way that ordinary hazard mitigation is usually promulgated, which has actually enticed development in hazardous areas. For example, the presence of dikes and levees in New Orleans gave residents a feeling of false security. Many similar examples have led to the general trend of fewer disaster events, but the ones now taking place have relatively much larger damages. Smart growth has tended to avoid such outcomes. Mileti (1999) has stated that "no single approach to bringing sustainable hazard mitigation into existence shows more promise at this time than increased use of sound and equitable land use management."

Burby et al. (2000) identify four major themes related to integrating mitigation into land-use planning in promoting community resilience, but only one of them, and only in part, pertains to the post-disaster period. This is an example of the tension in the planning field about terminology, similar to the discussion in other fields. Godschalk (2003; p. 137) concludes that "Traditional hazard mitigation programs have focused on making physical systems resistant to disaster forces." He goes on to state, however, that "future mitigation programs must also focus on teaching the city's social communities and institutions to reduce hazard risk and respond effectively to disasters, because they will be the ones most responsible for building ultimate urban resilience." In fact, Geis (2000) has explicitly stated a preference for the term "disaster-resistance" with respect to planning themes and practices in this area, concluding it is more appropriate and attractive than is "disaster resilient." At the same time, other planners have come to apply the term "resilient" to the interaction of physical and social systems (Olshansky and Kartez 1998).

Godschalk (2003) makes the point, however, that "Resilient cities are constructed to be strong and flexible, rather than brittle and fragile." It is this flexibility (adaptability) that is the key to resilience as interpreted by others (e.g., Comfort 1999; Rose 2007; Zolli and Healy 2012). Foster (1997) interprets this in terms of coping with contingencies. He has put forth 31 principles for achieving resilience, among them in the general systems realm are such characteristics as "being" diverse, renewable, functionally redundant, with reserve capacity achieved through duplication, interchangeability, and interconnections." Godschalk summarizes the work of several researchers to identify eight categories of resilience responses, seven of which have been emphasized by Rose (2004, 2007) and in this report: redundant, diverse, efficient, autonomous, strong, adaptable, and collaborative. Finally, Godschalk proposes a more enlightened set of mitigation measures for social and institutional resilience through the reduction of business interruption impacts, though the specific policy instruments he mentions are limited to loans and general government assistance, rather than the self-motivated coping behavior emphasized by most other analysts.

References

Adger WN (2000) Social and ecological resilience: are they related? Prog Hum Geogr 24(3):247–364

Adger WN, Hughes TP, Folke C, Carpenter SR, Rockstrom J (2005) Social-ecological resilience to coastal disasters. Science 309:1036–1039

Alexander D (2013) Resilience and disaster risk reduction: an etymological journey. Nat Hazards Earth Syst Sci Discuss 1:1257–1284

Ayres R, Simonis U (1989) Industrial metabolism. United Nations Press, Tokyo

Bruneau M, Chang S, Eguchi R, Lee G, O'Rourke T, Reinhorn A, Shinozuka M, Tierney K, Wallace W, von Winterfeldt D (2003) A framework to quantitatively assess and enhance seismic resilience of communities. Earthq Spectra 19:733–752
Burby R, Deyle R, Godschalk D, Olshansky R (2000) Creating hazard resistant communities through land-use planning. Nat Hazards Rev 1(2):99–106
Chang S, Shinozuka M (2004) Measuring and improving the disaster resilience of communities. Earthq Spectra 20:739–755
Comfort L (1994) Risk and resilience: inter-organizational learning following the Northridge earthquake of 17 January 1994. J Conting Crisis Manag 2(3):157–170
Comfort L (1999) Shared risk: complex seismic response. Pergamon, New York
Daly H, Farley J (2004) Ecological economics. Island Press, Washington, DC
Dovers R, Handmer J (1992) Uncertainty, sustainability and change. Glob Environ Chang 2(4):262–276
Erickson K (1976) Loss of communality at Buffalo Creek. Am J Psychiatry 133:302–305
Flynn S (2008) America the resilient: defying terrorism and mitigating natural disasters. Foreign Aff 87(2):2
Foster H (1997) The Ozymandias principles: thirty-one strategies for surviving change. UBC Press, Victoria
Geis D (2000) By design: the disaster-resistant and quality-of-life community. Nat Hazards Rev 1(3):151–160
Giesecke JA, Burns WJ, Barrett A, Bayrak E, Rose A, Slovic P, Suher M (2012) Assessment of the regional economic impacts of catastrophic events: CGE analysis of resource loss and behavioral effects of an RDD attack scenario. Risk Anal 32(4):583–600
Gigerenzer G, Selten R (eds) (2002) Bounded rationality: the adaptive toolbox. MIT Press, Cambridge, MA
Godschalk D (2003) Urban hazard mitigation: creating resilient cities. Nat Hazards Rev 4(3):136–143
Handmer JW, Dovers SR (1996) A typology of resilience: rethinking institutions for sustainable development. Organ Environ 9(4):482–511
Hill R, Paton D (2005) Managing company risk and resilience through business continuity management. In: Paton D and Johnston D (eds) Disaster resilience: an integrated approach. Charles C Thomas Publishers, Ltd., Springfield, Illinois
Hobfoll S (1998) Stress, culture, and community: the psychology and philosophy of stress. Plenum, New York
Holling C (1973) Resilience and stability of ecological systems. Annu Rev Ecol Syst 4:1–23
Intergovernmental Panel on Climate Change (IPCC) (2007) Climate change 2007: mitigation of climate change. Working Group III contribution to the fourth assessment report of the IPCC. Cambridge University Press, Cambridge
Klein R, Nicholls R, Thomalla F (2003) Resilience to natural hazards: how useful is this concept? Environ Hazards 5:35–45
Linkov I, Eisenberg D, Plourde K, Seager T, Allen J, Kott A (2013) Resilience metrics for cyber systems. Environ Syst Decis 33:471–476
Manyena S (2006) The concept of resilience revisited. Disasters 30(4):433–450
Meshkati N, Yalda K (2015) Operators' improvisation in complex technological systems: successfully tackling ambiguity, enhancing resiliency and the last resort to averting disaster. J Conting Crisis Manag 23(2):90–96
Mileti D (1999) Disasters by design: a reassessment of natural hazards in the United States. Joseph Henry Press, Washington, DC
Norris F, Friedman M, Watson P (2002) 60,000 disaster victims speak: part II, summary and implications of the disaster mental help research. Psychiatry 65:240–260
Norris F, Stevens S, Pfefferbaum V, Whyche K, Pfefferbaum R (2008) Community resilience as a metaphor, theory, set of capacities and strategy for disaster readiness. Am J Community Psychol 41:127–150

Olshansky R, Kartez J (1998) Managing land use to build resilience. In: Burby R (ed) Cooperating with nature: confronting natural hazards with land-use planning for sustainable communities. Joseph Henry Press, Washington, DC

Paton D, Johnston D (2001) Disasters and communities: vulnerability, resilience and preparedness. Disaster Prev Manag 10:270–277

Perrings C (2001) Resilience and sustainability. In: Folmer H, Gabel HL, Gerking S, Rose A (eds) Frontiers of environmental economics. Edward Elgar, Cheltenham

Pfefferbaum B, Reissman D, Pfefferbaum R, Klomp R, Gurwitch R (2005) Building resilience to mass trauma events. In: Doll L, Bonzo S, Mercy J, Sleet D (eds) Handbook on injury and violence prevention interventions. Kluwer Academic Publishers, New York

Pimm SL (1991) The balance of nature. University of Chicago Press, Chicago

Resilience Alliance (2005) Research on social–ecological systems: a basis for sustainability. http://www.resilience.org

Rose A (2004) Defining and Measuring Economic Resilience to Disasters. Disaster Prev Manag 13:307–314

Rose A (2007) Economic resilience to natural and man-made disasters: multidisciplinary origins and contextual dimensions. Environ Hazards 7(4):383–395

Rose A, Liao S (2005) Modeling resilience to disasters: computable general equilibrium analysis of a water service disruption. J Reg Sci 45(1):75–112

Rose A, Oladosu G, Lee B, Beeler-Asay G (2009) The economic impacts of the 2001 terrorist attacks on the World Trade Center: a computable general equilibrium analysis. Peace Econ Peace Sci Public Policy 15(2):Article 4

Rosoff H, Siko R, John R, Burns W (2013) Should I stay or should I go? An experimental study of health and economic government policies following a severe biological agent release. Environ Syst Decisions 33(1):121–137

Tierney K (1997) Impacts of recent disasters on businesses: the 1993 Midwest floods and the 1994 Northridge Earthquake. In: Jones B (ed) Economic consequences of earthquakes: preparing for the unexpected. National Center for Earthquake Engineering Research, Buffalo, pp 189–222

United Nations International Strategy for Disaster Reduction (UN/ISDR) (2002) Living with risk: a global review of disaster reduction initiatives by the ISDR. United Nations, Geneva

Zolli A, Healy AM (2012) Resilience: why things bounce back. Free Press, New York

Chapter 4
Economic Resilience

4.1 Basic Concepts

Resilience has four roles in the economics literature. Most generally, it is noted as an attribute of the economy in studies of economic shocks (see, e.g., Dhawan and Jeske 2006). In ecological economics, it is a major focus of analysis as a key attribute necessary for sustainability (see, e.g., Folke 2006). Some attempts have been made to extend this research to the socioeconomic arena and have it overlap with the study of institutions (see, e.g., Levin 1998). In the disaster literature, it has been an important dimension of hazard economic loss estimation and terrorist consequence analysis (Rose 2009a). Following Rose (2004, 2009b), we offer the following definitions of resilience to disasters:

Static Economic Resilience – The ability of a system to maintain function when shocked. This is the heart of the economic problem, where ordinary scarcity is made even more severe than usual, and it is imperative to use the remaining resources as efficiently as possible at any given point in time during the course of recovery.

Dynamic Economic Resilience – The ability to hasten the speed of recovery from a shock. This refers to the efficient utilization of resources for repair and reconstruction. Static resilience pertains to making the best of the existing capital stock (productive capacity), while this aspect is all about enhancing capacity. As such, it is about dynamics, in that it is time-related. Investment decisions involve diverting resources from consumption today in order to reap future gains from enhanced production.[1]

[1] Cutter (2016) has offered some different definitions of static and dynamic in a more general resilience context. She refers to dynamic properties in terms of resilience as a *process* and static conditions as relating to measurable *outcomes*. This distinction is useful and is made in this volume. This is not so much difference in consistency between Cutter's definitions and mine, but a matter of emphasis. In this volume, I emphasize that resilience is a process and agree that it could be labeled as dynamic because process is performed over time. However, the focus of this volume is on post-disaster implementation of the improved resilience capacity that the process engenders. Outcomes, however, can be either static or dynamic. If examined in the context of the influence of actions at a given point in time, and mathematical and economic terms, they would be characterized

A. Rose, *Defining and Measuring Economic Resilience from a Societal, Environmental and Security Perspective*, Integrated Disaster Risk Management,
DOI 10.1007/978-981-10-1533-5_4

Note that the definitions are couched in terms of function, typically measured in economics as the *flow* of goods and services, such as Gross Domestic Product (GDP) or broader measures of human well-being, as opposed to property damage. It is not the property (capital *stock*) that directly contributes to economic well-being but rather the flows that emanate from these stocks either for businesses or households. Two things should be kept in mind. First, while property damage takes place at a point in time, the reduced flow, often referred to on the production side as business interruption (BI), just begins at the time of the disaster but continues until the system has recovered or has attained a "new normal." Second, the recovery process, and hence the application of resilience depends heavily on the behavior of economic decision-makers and on public policy. Of course, recovery is a multi-faceted activity. It is not as simple as, for example, rebuilding a school destroyed by an earthquake, hurricane, or armed attack. Considerations must also be made of obstacles keeping children from returning to educational pursuits out of fear for their safety or the need to help their family earn a living.

Ability implies a level of attainment will be achieved. Hence, the definitions of economic resilience are contextual – the level of function has to be compared to the level that would have existed had the ability been absent. This means a reference point or path must be established. In the case of static economic resilience it refers to the worst case outcome. In the case of dynamic resilience it refers to the normal recovery path. Further discussion of this oft-neglected point is provided below.

Another important distinction is between *inherent* and *adaptive* resilience.[2] The former refers to aspects of resilience already built into the system before the

---

as static; however, if examined in terms of their effects over time, they typically would be referred to as dynamic in these disciplines.

[2]Geographer Cutter (2016) and I also differ on the meaning of *inherent* and *adaptive* resilience. She refers to the former as pertaining to baseline conditions, with the implication that these refer to pre-disaster, and the latter as pertaining to the post-disaster context. Again, this is less a matter of differences than emphasis. The definition of inherent resilience refers to the fact that it is already embodied in the economy (and broader community), but focuses on implementation of these capabilities after the disaster strikes. As to adaptive resilience, Cutter refers to it as the ability "... to learn from and respond to changes precipitated by some hazard event (p. 744)." In this volume, we emphasize that adaptive resilience refers to ingenuity or improvisation, which can be stimulated by a learning process but is not necessarily limited to that stimulus. The response aspect pertains to both static and dynamic resilience in this volume.

Sociologist Tierney (2014; p. 173) makes distinctions between inherent and adaptive resilience that also differ somewhat from those presented in this volume. She states: "the concept of inherent resilience refers to conditions, characteristics, and properties of analytic units that are associated with absorptive capacity that can potentially be mobilized to enhance coping capacity when disasters occur. Adaptive resilience involves the activation of that potential and actual disaster situations were strategies that overcome disaster induced problems as they manifest themselves." Tierney's definition of adaptive resilience is nearly the same as that presented in this volume. However, her definition of inherent resilience is broader and refers not only to its role in bouncing back, but also in relation to the resilience properties of resistance, robustness and redundancy, the latter two being half of the four cornerstones of the framework presented by Bruneau et al. (2003), to which Tierney was one of the contributors. Robustness refers to the ability to withstand a shock, and resistance typically is accorded the same definition or the slightly more subtle additional meaning of being able to deflect it. They are only indirectly related to bouncing back. Redundancy is an inherent aspect of resilience in the framework in this volume as well, however.

disaster, such as the availability of inventories, excess capacity, substitutability between inputs, contingent contractual arrangements accessing suppliers of goods from outside the affected area (imports), and the workings of the market system in allocating resources to their highest value use on the basis of price signals. Adaptive resilience arises out of improvisation under stress, such as Draconian conservation otherwise not thought possible (e.g., working many weeks without heat or air conditioning), changes in the way goods and services are produced, and new contracting arrangements that match customers who have lost their suppliers with suppliers who have lost their customers.

We analyze resilience pertaining to the economy at three levels:

- Microeconomic (individual business or household)
- Mesoeconomic (individual industry or market)
- Macroeconomic (combination of all economic entities, including their interactions)

4.2 Microeconomic Resilience

We present a conceptual framework for an analysis of economic resilience at the micro level based on economic production theory, an abstract approach to how businesses combine various inputs to produce outputs to sell to consumers. The framework is readily extended to how businesses interact in supply chains (meso level), and in one approach, known as computable general equilibrium (CGE) analysis, the economy is viewed as a set of integrated supply chains (macro level). The operation of businesses is still the focus of this approach, but their role in backward and forward linkages with other businesses can be examined in the context of the entire economy. Interestingly no resilience index in any discipline of the social sciences today has provided a formal conceptual framework. We note that our approach emanates from mainstream (neoclassical) economics, which is not without its limitations. It is often criticized for relying too much on optimizing behavior and equilibrium concepts. Below, we note how it can be adapted to overcome some of these limitations.

Business resilience has two sides. Customer-side resilience copes with the disruption (quantity and timing) of the delivery of inputs, and pertains to ways to use resources available as effectively as possible by both businesses and households, i.e., it is primarily associated with static resilience. For example, at a given point in time, meaning with a given fixed capital stock, in the context of electricity, or any critical input supply disruption, resilience is mainly a demand-side issue. In contrast, supply-side resilience is concerned with delivering outputs to customers, and could include the establishment of system redundancy (a form of static resilience), but usually requires the repair or construction of critical inputs (i.e. dynamic resilience). Repairs of the capital stock, or supply-side efforts, are the domain of the input provider and are a completely separate matter from customer-side resilience.

Government has both demand-side and supply-side resilience features in a manner similar to business. Of course, government at various levels plays a key role in economic recovery, so this is an added dimension of resilience in this sphere. Improvements in the quality and quantity of emergency services can be thought of as resilience enhancement. Increases in financial or in-kind disaster assistance and the effectiveness of their distribution to the affected parties promote recovery as well. However, the provision of aid can have disincentive effects on resilience, just as it does for mitigation, when those who suffer from a disaster because they have not undertaken mitigation are "bailed out."

In addition to customer-side resilience, households have supply-side resilience considerations with respect to providing their own services (e.g., cooking to prepare meal) or providing labor. However, household activities are not counted in national income accounts and are difficult to value, so supply-side resilience is less meaningful for households, and we have not included a separate table for it.

Resilience options for business are summarized in Tables 4.1 and 4.2 following Rose (2009b). Each table lists a major category of resilience and provides examples. Each specifies a prior action that can be taken to enhance each type of resilience. Each table also specifies the extent to which the resilience category is inherent and adaptive. In addition, the applicability of the type of resilience to factors of production is specified in terms of the letters capital (K), labor (L), infrastructure (I), materials (M), as well as for the output (Q) that they produce. Finally, obstacles to the implementation of each type of resilience are listed. Capital letters associated with each of these inputs or outputs represent a strong relationship, while lower-case letters represent a weak one. The same convention is used to denote the strength of inherent or adaptive resilience which is denoted by the letter X. For example, a firm can readily import all inputs except infrastructure services and physical capital, which are more limited because of their stationarity For example, factories cannot readily be relocated but equipment can be; thus these variables are relevant to relocation resilience, but are limited and hence connoted by lower case letters. Another example is that inherent conservation is primarily already accounted for by maximizing behavior, but we include it as at least weak, because not all firms actually maximize their production relationships.

For example, Table 4.1 presents resilience strategies for businesses on the customer side. The first category is Conservation and examples include automated controls to monitor the flow of inputs (e.g., water) to help make sure they are used only in times when they are needed and the reduction of non-essential uses. Prior action can be taken to promote resilience by closing systems to promote recycling, such as in the re-use of circulating water. Conservation is only minimally inherent because economists typically assume that most inherent conservation options are currently being maximized. Thus, most conservation options pertain to adaptive applications. All inputs–capital, labor, infrastructure services, and materials– can be conserved. The major obstacle is necessity of the input into the production process. Similar explanations are provided for other resilience options for the case of business customers.

Analogously, Table 4.2 presents resilience options on the business supplier side. This includes a different set of resilience categories in several cases. For example,

Table 4.1 Resilience options: business (customer-side)

Category	Prior action	Inherent[a]	Adaptive[a]	Applicability[a]	Obstacles
Conservation	Close system to promote recycling	x	X	K, L, I, M	Necessity
Automated controls					
Reduce non-essential					
Input substitution	Enhance flexibility of system	X	X	K, L, I, M	Specialization
Back-up generators					
Cross-training					
Import substitution	Broaden supply chain	X	X	k, L, i, M	Transportation
Mutual aid agreements					
Re-routing of goods					
Inventories (Stockpiles)	Enhance; protect	X	x	k, L, i, M	Storage capacity
Fuel supplies					
Labor pool					
Excess capacity	Build and maintain	X	x	K	Dilapidation
System redundancy					
Factor-in risk					
Input unimportance	Reduce dependence on critical inputs	X	X	K, l, I, M	Integrated process
Decrease dependence					
Segment production					
Relocation	Arrange for facilities in advance	x	X	K, L, I, M	Coordination
Back-up data centers					
Physical move					

(continued)

Table 4.1 (continued)

Category	Prior action	Inherent[a]	Adaptive[a]	Applicability[a]	Obstacles
Production recapture	Arrange long-term agreements	X	X	Q	Capacity
Information clearinghouse					
Restarting procedures					
Technological change	Increase flexibility	x	X	K, L, I, M, Q	Lack of ingenuity
Change processes					
Alter product characteristics					
Management effectiveness	Train; increase versatility	X	X	k, L, m	Pressure
Emergency procedures					
Succession/ continuity					

[a]Lower case letter indicates minor role

delivery logistics refers to the fact that suppliers must deliver their products to customers. Examples include shoring up the network of wholesale and retail trade, contingency contracts with transportation companies, and planning exercises. The rubric for prior action is "broadening the supply chain." These actions are strong at both the inherent and adaptive levels. As with most cases of supply-side resilience, they are applicable primarily to output. The major obstacle in implementing supplier-side resilience is the condition of the transportation network.

The inputs into economic activity noted in Table 4.1 serve as the independent variables for a formal production function in which the influence of several types of resilience can be linked directly to them or to the production function parameters. For example, Rose and Liao (2005) have shown how conservation is linked to the productivity term, and how input and import substitution are linked to the elasticities of substitution of a constant elasticity of substitution (CES) production function.

The production theory framework presented above reflects mainstream economics, but has its limitations (e.g., assuming maximizing behavior and a limited number of explanatory factors). It is intended as a starting point and can be enhanced by incorporating features of the behavioral theory of the firm (e.g., non- optimizing behavior and more managerial considerations) and bounded rationality in general (considerations of limited time horizons, limited information and limited ability to process it). One way to do this is to add a managerial term to the production function.

Many of the same resilience strategies associated with businesses and government are applicable to households. Following Rose (2009b), economic resilience options for households are summarized in Table 4.3 in a manner analogous to that presented for businesses, except the focus in this case is exclusively on the customer side.

Table 4.2 Resilience options: business (supplier-side)

Category	Prior action	Inherent[a]	Adaptive[a]	Applicability[a]	Obstacles
Delivery logistics	Broaden supply chain	X	X	Q	Transportation
Shore-up network of wholesale/retail trade					
Contingency contracts w/ transport companies					
Export substitution	Enhance flexibility	X	X	Q	Transportation
Expand markets					
Re-routing					
Inventories (Stockpiles)	Enhance	X	x	Q	Storage capacity
Strengthen storage facilities					
Pooling of resources					
Excess capacity	Build and maintain	X	X	K	Dilapidation
System redundancy					
Factor-in risk					
Relocation	Arrange for facilities in advance	x	X	K, L, I, M	Coordination
Move closer to customers					
Field operations					
Production recapture	Arrange long-term agreements	X	X	Q	Capacity
In relation to customer needs					
Practice restarting					
Technological change	Increase flexibility	x	X	K, L, I, M, Q	Ingenuity
Change processes					
Alter product characteristics					

(continued)

Table 4.2 (continued)

Category	Prior action	Inherent[a]	Adaptive[a]	Applicability[a]	Obstacles
Management effectiveness	Increase versatility	X	X	Q	Pressure
Project demand change					
Prioritize goods & services					
Reduce operating impediments	Recovery planning	x	X	K, L, I, M	Cognition
Assist family workers					
Streamline paperwork					

[a]Lower case letter indicates minor role

Table 4.3 Resilience strategies for households

Category	Prior action	Inherent[a]	Adaptive[a]	Applicability[a]	Obstacles
Conservation	Change habits	x	X	I,M	Necessity
Reduce non-essentials					
Belt tightening					
Input substitution	Enhance flexibility	X	X	L,I,M	Specialization
Back-up generators					
Blankets/flashlights/radio					
Import substitution	Broaden markets	X	X	k, L, i, M	Transportation
Cross-regional shopping					
E-shopping					
Inventories	Enhance and protect	X	x	k, L, i, M	Storage capacity
Stockpile food & fuel					
Pool resources					
Excess capacity	Build and maintain	X	x	K	Dilapidation
Redundancy (in place)					
Relocation	Improve social network	x	X	K, L, I, M	Coordination
Physical move					
Off-site data storage					

(continued)

Table 4.3 (continued)

Category	Prior action	Inherent[a]	Adaptive[a]	Applicability[a]	Obstacles
Activity recapture	Emergency exercises	x	x	Q	Capacity
Defer to later date					
Technological change	Increase flexibility	x	x	K, L, I, M, Q	Ingenuity
Change patterns					
Change equipment					
Management effectiveness	Designate leader	X	X	L	Pressure
Emergency procedures					
Organization					

[a]Lower case letter indicates minor role

For example, a household can readily import all inputs except infrastructure services and physical capital, which are less amenable to this tactic because of their stationarity. Another example is that inherent conservation is primarily already accounted for by maximizing behavior, but we include it as at least weak, because not all households actually maximize their "production" relationships. Thus, most conservation options pertain to adaptive applications. All inputs–capital, labor, infrastructure services, and materials–can be conserved, but the moderating factor is the necessity of the input into the household production process or functioning.

4.3 Meso and Macro Resilience

At the mesoeconomic level, resilience options aim at bolstering the market or sectors and include, for instance, pricing mechanisms, industry pooling of resources and information, and sector-specific types of infrastructure such as railways. What is often less appreciated by disaster researchers outside economics and closely related disciplines is the inherent resilience of market prices that act as the "invisible hand" to guide resources to their best allocation in the aftermath of a disaster. Some pricing mechanisms have been established expressly to deal with such a situation, as in the case of non-interruptible service premiums that enable customers to estimate the value of a continuous supply of electricity and to pay in advance for receiving priority service during an outage. The price mechanism is a relatively costless guide to redirecting goods and services. Price increases, to the extent that they do not reflect "gouging," serve a useful purpose of reflecting highest value use, even in the broader social setting. Moreover, if the allocation does violate principles of equity (fairness), the market allocations can be adjusted by income or material transfers to the needy. Of course, markets are likely to be damaged by a major disaster, in an analogous manner to buildings and humans. In this case, we have two alternatives for some or all of the economy in a manner similar to addressing market failures under normal circumstances of externalities, public goods, and market power: (1) substitute centralized decree or planning, though at a significantly higher cost of administration; (2) bolster the market, such as by improving information flows (e.g., the creation of an information clearinghouse to match customers without suppliers to suppliers without customers). Both approaches are forms of resilience.

At the macroeconomic level, resilience is very much influenced by interdependencies between sectors. Consequently, macroeconomic resilience is not only a function of resilience measures implemented by single businesses, but it is also determined by the actions taken by all individual companies and markets including their interaction (see Martin and Sunley 2014). Examples of resilience options at the macro-level would be, e.g., economic diversity to buffer impacts on individual sectors, or geographic proximity to economies not affected by disaster to facilitate access to goods or aid. Others include fiscal (e.g., infrastructure spending to boost the affected economy) and monetary policy (e.g., keeping interest rates low to stimulate private sector reinvestment). The macro level overlaps with the popular focus on "community resilience" and represents a more holistic picture. However, economists have long appreciated the importance of microeconomic foundations of macroeconomic analysis for several reasons. First, the macroeconomy is composed of individual building blocks of producer and consumer behavior as underpinnings for macroeconomic considerations stemming from group interactions. Second, behavioral considerations are best addressed first at the most elemental level because of the prominence of individual motivations for survival and coping mechanisms in anticipation of and in response to disasters.

References

Bruneau M, Chang S, Eguchi R, Lee G, O'Rourke T, Reinhorn A, Shinozuka M, Tierney K, Wallace W, von Winterfeldt D (2003) A framework to quantitatively assess and enhance seismic resilience of communities. Earthq Spectra 19:733–752

Cutter S (2016) The landscape of disaster resilience indicators in the USA. Nat Hazards 80:741–758

Dhawan R and Jeske K (2006) How resilient is the modern economy to energy price shocks? Econ Rev, Federal Reserve Bank of Atlanta, Third Quarter, pp 21–32.

Folke C (2006) Resilience: the emergence of a perspective for social–ecological systems analyses. Glob Environ Chang 16(3):253–267

Levin S (1998) Resilience in natural and socioeconomic systems. Environ Dev Econ. Special Issue on Resilience and Sustainability 3(2):221–235

Martin R, Sunley P (2014) The notion of regional economic resilience: conceptualization and explanation. J Econ Geogr 15(1):1–42

Rose A (2004) Defining and measuring economic resilience to disasters. Disaster Prev Manag 13:307–314

Rose A (2009a) A framework for analyzing and estimating the total economic impacts of a terrorist attack and natural disaster. J Homeland Secur Emerg Manag 6(1):6
Rose A (2009b) Economic resilience to disasters. Community and Resilience Institute Research Report Number 8. ORNL
Rose A, Liao S (2005) Modeling resilience to disasters: computable general equilibrium analysis of a water service disruption. J Reg Sci 45(1):75–112
Tierney K (2014) The social roots of risk: producing disasters, promoting resilience. Stanford University Press, Stanford, CA

Chapter 5
Broader Dimensions of Economic Resilience

5.1 Commonalities with Other Disciplines

Overall, there are more commonalities than differences in the various definitions of resilience. All definitions relate to reducing losses from disasters. All emanate from a survival motivation. Nearly all emphasize the importance of adaptive behavior. Most view resilience as a process and emphasize the need to expand resilience capacity at multiple levels. Most emphasize interactions within a broader community. Most stress the importance of natural, societal and/or produced resources and their wise utilization in a crisis. Moreover, there are few inconsistencies between the definitions. They differ mainly in terms of some unique terrain they stake out from their own discipline. This is one of the reasons we have chosen a broad definition of resilience at the outset. It is better to consider the union of the various sets of definitions, as opposed to just their intersection, in order to capture all of the potential benefits of his important concept when made operational as a strategy to reduce losses. Cutter (2016) has noted that it is the integration of the various disciplines in resilience analysis that is deficient. She suggests that it is the spatial sciences that hold the most promise in this regard.

The various disciplines also point to the need for structural change to overcome obstacles to human development and the building of resilience capacity. For example, discrimination against women and minorities requires changes in attitudes and institutions to promote concepts of equality. Changes are required in land-use planning, insurance, and banking to decrease moral hazard to make people aware of the full implications of their decisions to live and build in high-risk areas. This process can be facilitated by improving the workings of markets to include the full social costs of actions, such as using pollution taxes or security premiums, or by removing subsidies that are simply based on political influence rather than desirable goals, and then by providing new subsidies for worthy goals, such as the purchase of disaster insurance.

A. Rose, *Defining and Measuring Economic Resilience from a Societal, Environmental and Security Perspective*, Integrated Disaster Risk Management,
DOI 10.1007/978-981-10-1533-5_5

5.2 Multiple Dimensions

We now summarize the many dimensions of *economic resilience* more broadly:

- *Multi-scale*. The concept of resilience is applicable at multiple scales, from the resilience of an individual person (e.g., psychological, financial) to that of an organization, neighborhood, city, or nation.
- *Multi-hazard*. Resilience pertains to all hazards and not just earthquakes. Moreover, resilience to other hazards can in many cases be applied to earthquakes.
- *Stocks* (property damage) *and flows* (production of goods and services) of assets, systems, economies, and communities. Property damage takes place at a given point in time, but the service flows (to which maintaining function applies) are disrupted until recovery is completed, and are thus more central to the idea of rebounding after a disaster.
- *Behavior and policy*. The length of the recovery following disasters is not some constant that can be known beforehand, but an outcome that depends critically on decisions and activities undertaken by private and public sector decision makers.
- *Geophysical*. Resilience generally varies inversely to the size of the shock to the system.
- *Bifurcation of temporal aspects*. Static resilience refers to the ability of an entity or system to maintain function when shocked and relates to how to efficiently allocate the resources remaining after the disaster. Dynamic resilience refers to the speed at which an entity or system recovers from a shock and is a relatively more complex problem because it involves a long-term investment associated with repair and reconstruction.
- *Context*. The level of function of the system at a point in time has to be compared to the level that would have existed had the ability been absent, requiring that a reference point or worst-case outcome be established first.
- *Capacity*. *Inherent* resilience refers to the ordinary ability already in place to deal with crises. *Adaptive* resilience refers to ability in crisis situations to maintain function on the basis of ingenuity or extra effort.
- *Market*. This refers to the need to consider both the providers and customers of building and infrastructure services in moving toward a holistic definition of resilience
- *Cost*. Resilience essentially represents a measure of benefits of various actions. However, the cost side cannot be neglected in policy decisions.
- *Process*. Resilience is not just about actions and targets; the manner in which these are achieved is a critical aspect. This refers to developing and applying a set of adaptive capacities.
- *Fairness*. Resilience should be applied in an equitable manner, to be sensitive to the needs of the most disadvantaged groups in society with care being taken to avoid having any group adversely affected by its implementation.

5.3 Vulnerability and Resilience

Timmerman (1981) and others also relate resilience to *vulnerability*. Some have contended that resilience and vulnerability are opposites, while others see them as interrelated (Manyena 2006). Specifically, Pelling (2003) decomposes vulnerability to natural hazards into three parts: exposure, resistance, and resilience. Cutter and others have developed extensive vulnerability indices composed of many variables, many of them longer-term background conditions such as percent minority (as well as women and infirm), per capita income (see, e.g., Cutter et al. 2003). As does Blaikie et al. (1994), Pelling defines resilience to natural hazards as the ability of an individual or community to cope with or adapt to hazard stress. An alternative view is that vulnerability is primarily a pre-disaster condition, but that resilience is the outcome of a post-disaster response. Resilience is one of several ways to reduce vulnerability, the others being adaptation and the mitigation.

Many areas of the world are more vulnerable to threats to their security than others. For example, large cities are vulnerable to disasters for a number of reasons. First they represent large concentrations of population in the built environment, including complex infrastructure. This concentration makes them more susceptible to contagion effects associated with the spread of disease, fire, and building collapse. Concentration also makes evacuation in anticipation of disasters more difficult. The complexity of cities stems primarily from their overall interdependence and the more sophisticated nature of economic and social activity than in other areas. Together with the faster pace of life, this makes cities relatively rigid, thus leading to less flexibility and hence less resilience. The economic rationale for cities in the first place often places them in more highly vulnerable locations, such as along coasts or major rivers. They represent larger targets for terrorists as well. In the case of major disasters, the very size of cities makes them more likely to be overwhelmed by large disasters in providing emergency response services, such as fire and health care.

Despite their overall and per capita wealth, cities typically also house large percentages of low-income and other disadvantaged population groups. These groups have higher vulnerability to temperature extremes and susceptibility/mortality to vector-borne diseases, whose spread has been linked to higher temperatures and moisture levels. These groups also have lower resilience capacities than others in terms of education, social connectivity, material resources, and political clout.

At the same time, cities also have some distinct advantages with respect to resilience. They are relatively more diversified economically, and thus more likely to be able to withstand a severe shock to any given sector. While overall they may not have a higher proportion of excess capacity at a given point in time than population centers of other sizes, cities have a greater absolute amount of excess capacity to absorb displaced businesses and residents when the disaster is not widespread. They also contain a greater amount of other resources for recovery and reconstruction, as well as more specialized skills and expertise. Cities typically are centers of innovation, a key ingredient of resilience. Cities are also likely to have greater prominence and political power, and thus are able to command greater transfers of resources from outside their boundaries. They are likely to be characterized by stronger social networks as well. At the same time, all of the examples just provided are effective up to some threshold, at which point resilience can be overwhelmed. In these cases the sheer size of the city becomes a liability.

Several striking examples exist of the grand resilience of cities, including the rapid rebuilding following the Lisbon earthquake of 1700, Chicago fire of 1876, San Francisco earthquake of 1906, Hiroshima atomic bomb attack of 1945, and Mexico City earthquake of 1985. This also includes the enormous resilience of the New York City area following the September 11, 2001, terrorist attacks, where 95 % of the businesses and government agencies located in the World Trade Center area were able to relocate relatively rapidly nearby because of the large supply of excess office space (Rose et al. 2009). New Orleans is an excellent example of a city whose resilience was overwhelmed by a major hurricane and induced technological failure that resulted in massive flooding. Subsequently, however, New Orleans, which lost a large percentage of its population from Hurricane Katrina, perhaps permanently, has had its downtown and tourist business cores rebound because of the strong demand for goods and services produced there (Robertson 2009).

5.4 Sustainability and Resilience

Several ecologists and ecological economists have linked resilience to the concept of *sustainability*, which refers to long-term progress and survival without diminishing the quality of life for future generations. Common (1995) suggests that resilience is the key to this concept. A major feature of sustainability is that it is highly dependent on natural resources, including the environment. Destroying, damaging, or depleting resources undercuts longer-term economic viability, a lesson also applicable to natural hazard impacts, where most analysts have omitted ecological considerations. Klein et al. (2003) note that, from an economic perspective, sustainability is a function of the degree to which key hazard impacts are anticipated. Others take the position that it is also a function of a society's ability to react effectively to a crisis, and with minimal reliance on outside resources (see Mileti 1999; IFRC 2004).

What is the relationship between resilience and sustainability? Resilience is usually used in the context of responding to specific shocks, and thus relates to short-run survival and recovery. This contributes to long-run survival, a key aspect of sustainability along with improving the quality of life and the environment. However, the distinction is blurred in several key ways:

- Resilience in the short-run can be carried over to adaptation in the long-run.
- Disasters open up opportunities to rebuild and improve outcomes, including mitigating against future disasters.

- Disasters provide a valuable learning experience of how to cope with extreme stress.
- Disasters provide outside economic stimulus to the affected economy through insurance and through private and public sector assistance.

Zolli and Healy (2012) have recently identified a major difference between resilience and sustainability that is especially important in relation to climate change. They view resilience focusing on disequilibrium situations and stability, in contrast to sustainability's focus on equilibrium paths. They point to the need for a re-orientation of infrastructure being designed to be less brittle and more robust, and overall more flexible so as to be able to rebound. The authors point out that many practices promoting sustainability do not necessarily promote resilience. A key example is new energy-efficient buildings, which include systems that promote longevity but not necessarily the ability to withstand or rebound from shocks. Zolli and Healy also point to the importance of eco-systems in our future ability to deal with disasters to humankind. They point to the fact that the extensive flooding associated with Hurricane Katrina was due in part to deterioration of wetlands to the south and east of the city. These natural barriers were destroyed by human development, and this is just one of many examples of so-called progress being neither sustainable nor resilient.

5.5 Adaptation and Resilience

In the context of longer-term disasters, such as climate change, Timmerman (1981) defined resilience as the measure of a system's capacity to absorb and recover from the occurrence of a hazardous event. In the climate change context, however, most researchers now refer to this as *adaptation* (see, e.g., IPCC 2007). Kates et al. (2012) argue that most of the on-going adaptation to climate change is incremental, but that this is likely to become increasingly insufficient, such that "transformational" adaptation (new to a region, larger and involving geographic shifts) will be needed. Dovers and Handmer (1992) note an important feature that distinguishes man from the rest of nature in this context – human capacity for anticipating and learning (see also Resilience Alliance 2005). They then bifurcate resilience into reactive and proactive, where the latter is uniquely human. Others maintain that proactive efforts can enhance resilience by increasing its capacity prior to a disaster, but that resilience is operative only in the response/recovery/reconstruction (often referred to as "post-disaster") stages (Rose 2009). Adaptability is not just applicable to long-term events, but is a major attribute of resilience to disasters. Moreover, this adaptability requires that we consider a revised equilibrium state in measuring stability and resilience. Most ecological economists view flexibility and adaptability as the essence of resilience (see, e.g., Levin et al. 1998). This makes intuitive sense for natural disasters as well given their uncertainty in terms of infrequency and consequences.

Adaptation can be viewed as the complement to mitigation in the long run. When disasters cannot be or are not mitigated, we typically resort to adaptation. For example, while mitigation of the causes of climate change is the preferred approach, the reality is that some amount of climate change is inevitable given the fact that greenhouse gases (GHGs) are "fund" pollutants (i.e., they have long residence times in the atmosphere, and hence any emissions in a given year add to the existing concentrations). Even large cutbacks in emissions will still result in an increased atmospheric concentration of GHGs (IPCC 2007). Thus, the second best response to climate change is adaptation – actions to minimize losses for the climate change that does occur (Mazmanian et al. 2010). Typically, adaptation is associated with long-term, or chronic, climate change, as opposed to short-term climate variability. There are as many adaptation strategies as there are resilience strategies, and many overlap. Examples of adaptation include the creation of drought-resistant crops, construction of seawalls, safeguards against wildfires, and population migration.

We begin with the hypothesis that resilience can be thought of as a short-run version of adaptation, geared toward dealing with disasters related to climate change. However, some subtle differences arise. Building a levee or a seawall mitigates riverine floods or ocean storm surge, but is an adaptation strategy with respect to climate change. Also, if resilience refers to bouncing back, population migration is the antithesis, though there is an increasing realization that the optimal recovery from the disaster is not necessarily to return to prior population and economic levels if they are not sustainable (see, e.g., New Orleans following Hurricane Katrina). Still, many ways of translating resilience into sustainable practices can also extend resilience to adaptation practices as well (see below).

One key institution relating to both resilience and adaptation is the market. Ideally, price signals would help allocate resources efficiently in response to a crisis. However, major disasters are likely to lead to severe market failures, owing to asymmetries of damage, myopia, and uncertainty. In the short-term, destruction of productive capacity leads to market disarray and the propensity for gouging that obscures market signals. In the case of adaptation, these signals are more likely to be obscured by lack of information and awareness of the risk. Economists have long emphasized market failure (including myopia, principal-agent problems, moral hazard) as an obstacle to dealing with disasters, in terms of why sufficient resources are not devoted to mitigation and why people do not purchase sufficient flood insurance (see, e.g., Kuneuther et al. 2013).

Equity is more complicated in the case of long-run climate change, since one needs to consider not only the fair sharing of costs and benefits within a given time period, but across generations. This dynamic, or intergenerational, equity issue is an especially thorny problem. The interest rate is a type of price that reflects the intertemporal tradeoffs in resource allocation. However, over long periods, any positive interest rate "discounts" future generations, and, if the rate is low enough or the time period long enough (e.g., in excess of 5 % or more than 50 years), the present value discounting essentially results in stipulating "future generations don't count" (see, e.g., Brennan 1999). One solution is to preserve present value discounting but to establish a set aside fund to enhance the capacity of future generations to adapt to climate change.

The application of resilience to dealing with short-run aspects of climate change is at an advanced stage in some ways and in its infancy in others. Yes, we have improved our resilience capacity with respect to individual hurricanes, floods, wildfires, and droughts. However, we have not necessarily witnessed the frequency and magnitude of such events that climate change portends. Nor are we adequately prepared for the simultaneous or compound events that are likely to occur in the future. And nor are we prepared for unprecedented or unknown short and long-term events that could emanate from climate change, such as flooding in locations that have never witnessed such events before or the "deep-freeze" prospect for Europe in case of a "flipping" of the North Atlantic conveyer-belt (responsible for the warm water ocean current flowing to this region).

References

Blaikie P, Cannon T, Davis I, Wisner B (1994) At risk: natural hazards, people's vulnerability and disasters. Routledge, London

Brennan T (1999) Discounting the future. The RFF reader. Resources for the Future, Washington, DC

Common M (1995) Sustainability and policy limits to economics. Cambridge University Press, Cambridge

Cutter S (2016) The landscape of disaster resilience indicators in the USA. Nat Hazards 80:741–758

Cutter S et al (2003) Social vulnerability to environmental hazards. Soc Sci Q 84(2):241–261

Dovers R, Handmer J (1992) Uncertainty, sustainability and change. Glob Environ Chang 2(4):262–276

Intergovernmental Panel on Climate Change (IPCC) (2007) Climate change 2007: mitigation of climate change. Working Group III contribution to the fourth assessment report of the IPCC. Cambridge University Press, Cambridge

International Federation of Red Cross and Red Crescent Societies (IFRC) (2004) World disasters report 2004: focus on community resilience. IFRC, Geneva

Kates R, Travis W, Wilbanks T (2012) Transformational adaptation when incremental adaptations to climate change are insufficient. Proc Natl Acad Sci 109(19):7156–7161

Klein R, Nicholls R, Thomalla F (2003) Resilience to natural hazards: how useful is this concept? Environ Hazards 5:35–45

Kuneuther H, Michel-Kerjan E, Pauly M (2013) Making America more resilient toward natural disasters: a call for action. Environment 55(4):15–23

Levin S et al (1998) Resilience in natural and socioeconomic systems. Environ Dev Econ. Special Issue on Resilience and Sustainability 3(2):221–235.

Manyena S (2006) The concept of resilience revisited. Disasters 30(4):433–450

Mazmanian D et al. (2010) Preparing for the effects of climate change – a strategy for California. A report of the California Adaptation Advisory Panel to the State of California. Pacific Council on International Policy

Mileti D (1999) Disasters by design: a reassessment of natural hazards in the United States. Joseph Henry Press, Washington, DC

Pelling M (2003) The vulnerability of cities: natural disasters and social resilience. London, Earthscan

Resilience Alliance (2005) Research on social–ecological systems: a basis for sustainability. http://www.resilience.org

Robertson C (2009) In New Orleans, recovery is not enough. New York Times. http:/www.nytimes.com/2009/08/31/us/31orleans.html

Rose A (2009) Economic resilience to disasters. Community and Resilience Institute Research Report Number 8. ORNL.

Rose A, Oladosu G, Lee B, Beeler-Asay G (2009) The economic impacts of the 2001 terrorist attacks on the World Trade Center: a computable general equilibrium analysis. Peace Econ Peace Sci Public Policy 15(2):4

Timmerman P (1981) Vulnerability, resilience and the collapse of society: a review of models and possible climatic applications. J Climatology 1(4):396–438

Zolli A, Healy AM (2012) Resilience: why things bounce back. Free Press, New York

Chapter 6
Measuring Economic Resilience

We illustrate the application of the definition of resilience with the following case study by Rose et al. (2009), who estimated the national and regional economic impact of the September 11, 2001, terrorist attack on the World Trade Center (WTC). The researchers refined some available data indicating that more than 95 % of the businesses and government offices operating in the WTC area survived by relocating; the vast majority to Mid-town Manhattan or across the river in Northern New Jersey. Had all of these firms gone out of business, the potential direct economic loss in terms of GDP would have been \$43 billion. However, relocation was not immediate, taking anywhere from a few days to as long as 8 months for the vast majority of firms. Rose et al. (2009) calculated this loss in GDP at \$11 billion. They were then able to apply the resilience definition provided in this chapter to estimate that the effectiveness of relocation as a resilience tactic in the aftermath of the 9/11 attacks was 72 % (\$43 minus \$11, divided by \$43). This study highlights the importance of excess capacity as a resilience tactic. This more intensive use of resources is also the theme of the recovery in the recent great recession in the U.S. and other countries, as employment recovery significantly lacks the recovery of output. The experience of New York City thus signals a significant change in approaches to disaster recovery, which typically emphasized prompt rebuilding. Coupled with stronger requirements for mitigation, and hopefully some general accumulated wisdom, we are recovering less by reflex action and more by intelligent planning (see also Valle and Campanella 2005; Chang and Rose 2012).

6.1 Temporal Aspects and Resilience Metrics

Figure 6.1 illustrates some of the features of resilience and related concepts overall and in relation to timing in particular. These include the normal time-path of a system like the economy, the initial ability to limit the consequences of a shock,

A. Rose, *Defining and Measuring Economic Resilience from a Societal, Environmental and Security Perspective*, Integrated Disaster Risk Management,
DOI 10.1007/978-981-10-1533-5_6

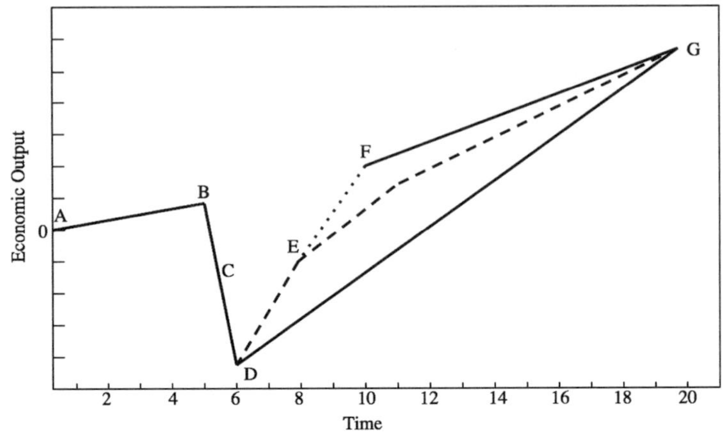

Fig. 6.1 The time-path of resilience

rebounding, and learning aspects, such that the system might even be able to attain a stronger growth path if recovery is undertaken properly.

Following Rose (2009b), Chang et al. (2011), and Petersen and Rose (2013), in Fig. 6.1 the vertical axis represents system performance, and the horizontal axis represents time. The performance increases starting at Point A until the system is hit by a shock at Point B. The shock causes it to degrade to a lower level at Point D. *Robustness* is a measure of the difference between the drop to the level at Point D and a maximum drop for the specific disaster, which we can, for the purpose of illustration, say is a zero performance level. Resilience is of two types depicted in relation to Points F and G. *Static resilience* begins at point D and refers to using the *remaining resources* to move to a higher level of performance during recovery. *Dynamic resilience* begins at point E and refers to the ability to recover more quickly by more effective *repair and reconstruction.* As a result of static resilience, the system recovers to its pre-disaster trajectory level at point G at best (it may not be able to return to the original path at all if investment in repair and reconstruction is not undertaken). Dynamic resilience, however, enables the system to recover earlier than it otherwise would have at point F. Further resilience can also refer to reconstruction that makes the system more robust for future disasters, or that represents the sustainability of adaptive resilience learning from the disaster just analyzed (not shown). Static resilience is the reduction in losses corresponding to the area (difference) between the base recovery path and the dashed arc (DEG). Dynamic resilience corresponds to the area (difference) between the dashed arc and the dotted and the solid line (EFG). An alternative measure of dynamic resilience would be the difference between a normal repair/reconstruction path and an accelerated one (Xie et al. 2016).

Resilience need not be monotonically increasing, meaning that the recovery path need not always be increasing. Also, resilience can be degraded or overwhelmed, causing dips in the recovery path, as in the case of Hurricane Katrina. The discussion above is most appropriate in relation to engineering and economic systems. It does not, however, adequately convey many aspects of resilience as a process, which is much more important in organizational and community resilience.

Following Rose (2004, 2009a), we provide an admittedly crude but operational metric of resilience. *Direct Static Economic Resilience* (*DSER*) refers to the level of the individual firm or industry (micro and meso levels) and corresponds to what economists refer to as "partial equilibrium" analysis, or the operation of a business or household entity itself. *Total Static Economic Resilience* (*TSER*) refers to the economy as a whole (macro level) and would ideally correspond to what is referred to as "general equilibrium" analysis, which includes all of the price and quantity interactions in the economy. The market itself, when functioning properly, is a major source of resilience at the meso and macro levels (see, e.g., Horwich 1995).

An operational measure of *DSER* is the extent to which the estimated direct output reduction deviates from the likely maximum potential reduction given an external shock, such as the curtailment of some or all of a critical input. In essence *DSER* is the percentage avoidance of the maximum economic disruption that a particular shock could bring about. A major measurement issue is what should be used as the maximum potential disruption. For ordinary disasters, a good starting point is a linear, or proportional, relationship between an input supply shortage and the direct disruption to the firm or industry. Note that while a linear reference point may appear to be arbitrary or a default choice, it does have an underlying rationale. A linear relationship connotes rigidity, the opposite of the "flexibility" connotation of static resilience defined in this paper. Analogously, the measure of *TSER* is the difference between a linear set of indirect effects, which implicitly omits resilience, and a non-linear outcome, which incorporates the possibility of resilience.

Also, while the entire time-path of resilience is a key to the concept for many analysts, it is important to remember that this time-path is composed of a sequence of individual steps. Even if "dynamics" are the focal point, it is important to understand the underlying process at each stage, i.e., why an activity level is achieved and why that level differs from one time period to another. As presented here, static resilience helps explain the first aspect, and changes in static resilience, along with repair and reconstruction of the capital stock, help explain the second.

Another way to view the temporal aspects of resilience in terms of stages of its applications to various dimensions is presented in Table 6.1.

6.2 Spatial Dimensions and Businesses

Most natural disasters take place at the local or regional level in large countries. Terrorist attacks, other than some cyber or than those that spread disease are localized as well, though they are intended to place an entire country or larger region in a state of fear, or to do injury to their broader economies. Climate change is of course global. These factors have implications for resilience and disaster recovery in general. For example, the more localized the event, other things being equal, the

Table 6.1 Resilience applications to social, ecological, physical, and economic recovery by time period

Timescale	Emergency response	Health & safety	Utilities	Buildings	Environmental/ecological	Economic
Immediate <72 h	Tactical emergency response	Deal with casualties/ reunite families	Use of emergency back-up systems	Remove debris	Limit further ecological damage	Maintain supply of critical goods & services
Emergency 3–7 days	Strategic emergency response	Provide mass care	Begin service restoration	Provide shelter for homeless	Remove debris	Prioritize use of resources/ substitute inputs/conserve
Very short 7–30 days	Selective response	Fight infectious outbreaks	Continue restoration	Provide shelter for homeless	Protect sensitive ecosystems	Shore-up or over-ride markets
Short 1–6 months	Assist in recovery	Deal with post-traumatic stress	Complete service restoration	Provide temporary housing and business sites	Deal with ensuing problems	Cope with small business strain
Medium 6 months–1 year	Reassess for future emergencies	Deal with post-traumatic stress	Reassess for future emergencies	Provide temporary housing and business sites	Initiate remediation	Cope with large business strain/recapture lost production
Long >1 year	n.a.	Reassess for future emergencies	Mitigation for future events	Rebuild & mitigation	Mitigation for future events	Cope with business failures/mitigation

greater the ability to draw upon resources (ranging from critical inputs to general population assistance) from the larger national pool.

In this chapter we discuss the spatial aspects of external shocks to an economy in general and illustrate them with special reference to insidious terrorist attacks, such as those caused by chemical, biological, radiological and nuclear mediums. Several valuable analyses have been performed but typically in a relatively aspatial manner. For example, Giesecke et al. (2012, 2015) in studies of a radiological ("dirty bomb" and chlorine gas attacks on the Los Angeles financial district identified the contaminated area as the site of the impacts and translated the impacts into changes in factor availability and prices for firms located there. This affects firm competitiveness and hence imports and exports of the LA economy as a whole by averaging the direct impacts across all firms in its County. But several other spatial aspects were omitted, some of which relate to economic resilience.

Following Giesecke et al. (2015), we provide an overview of a systematic framework for the spatial analysis of the impacts of a terrorist attack, primarily with the objective of improving the accuracy of the estimates of economic consequences. We also indicate how the inclusion of a broader set of spatial dimensions would affect the outcome. We begin by noting two special features of a chlorine attack that distinguish it from other types of disasters. The first relates to fear and stigma effects (see, e.g., Slovic 1987; Giesecke et al. 2012). Additionally, because of the uncertainty regarding the spread of chlorine gas or other insidious weapons whose dispersion is related to weather conditions and are difficult to detect, we should also consider that the fear/stigma will not halt abruptly at the financial district boundary. It is reasonable to consider a fringe zone where these behavioral considerations may spill over and have impacts, though likely less intensive than in the core area.

A behavioral consideration relates to the likelihood and pace of business relocation. The 9/11 example indicates that the response is likely to be rapid and not far from the original site. Both of these responses were conditioned somewhat upon broader aspects of resilience, in the form of demonstrating to terrorists that they cannot defeat their intended targets (Flynn 2008). There is every reason to believe that this "we will show them" attitude would prevail in LA as well.

A complication is that relocation may not be entirely out of the region for which the impact analysis was performed but may also take place within the region, as in the case of World Trade Center area firms moving to Midtown Manhattan. Also, business activity in cyberspace and tele-commuting have increased significantly in recent years, further blurring boundaries. Finally, there is the longstanding issue of the ready ability to shift economic activity among branch plants of the same company. Given all these considerations, a quarantine plus geographic averting behavior may not result in losses as great as initially predicted.

Below we discuss in detail various aspects of the potential spatial realignment of economic activity in relation to the chlorine attack scenario:

Business Relocation Alternatives First we must consider relocation out of the financial district. This would potentially include: (i) actual physical relocation; (ii) a shift of activity to other branches of the firm; and/or (iii) work primarily in cyberspace.

Physical relocation is likely to approach zero in a case where quarantine/decontamination lasts only a few days. Shift of activity to branch offices is a possibility, especially for firms involved in banking, finance and insurance. Work in cyber space, including tele-commuting, deserves special attention here because it is becoming more prevalent, especially in the banking and finance sectors that are predominant in the area affected by the attack. This activity may not be affected in any significant way. Increasingly, businesses are backing-up their systems such that even if main computers are located in the financial district, relevant files can be accessed from elsewhere. Similarly, data are being increasingly stored on various types of "cloud." The prevalence of these cyber options warrants adjustment of direct impact estimates when data become available.

We must also distinguish shifts of locations *within* LA County from those going elsewhere. As in the post-9/11 shift to Mid-town Manhattan, there are several advantages to relocating in close proximity to the original site. Doing so would not lead to any reduction in economic activity within LA County, all other things being equal. Of course, business relocation does have its costs. If it significantly increases the cost of doing business at the new location, this increased cost would have to be factored into the analysis, and would lower the level of economic activity in LA County by affecting its competitiveness.

Economic Activity Shift Out of the Region This aspect does not pertain to the actual physical movement of firms, but rather to their activity levels in place. It relates to an increase in their cost of doing business due to increased wage demands and increased investor rates of return to compensate for increased risk. It also relates to their likely reduced profits as they have to provide customer discounts. In the case of the later, the base for the activity shifts decreases (fewer firms to which to apply what are essentially declines in competiveness or product demand that lead to reduced sectoral output).

Temporal Dimension of Spatial Shifts It is important to distinguish between business relocation at various points in time. The implications of these decisions differ significantly for the consequence estimates between the initial contamination, clean-up, risk amplification, and stigma phases. While firms may not have time to physically relocate during the short-run response (decontamination), opportunities to do so increase over time, though the incentives to do so decline as well (see the discussion above of the decay rate for fear). Thus, some relocation decisions (including branch offices and cyber space activity) affect ordinary losses, and others affect behavioral losses

One also needs to consider the potential for a reverse movement of businesses. Abadie and Dermisi (2011) investigated the movement of many WTC area firms who left Lower Manhattan right after 9/11 but returned. The same phenomenon could take place for the type of terrorist attack that we have analyzed, though it is less likely because of (misplaced) fear of lingering contamination. One would also need to consider the extent to which the attack site is seen as a prime target for future attacks, contributing to persistent stigma.

Problems of spillovers of disasters across political boundaries are beyond the scope of this volume. However, advances are being made in inter-jurisdictional cooperation to deal with them, including the application of resilience tactics (Rose and Kustra 2013).

6.3 Spatial Dimensions and People

We turn now to the special case of those geographically displaced, possibly permanently, by crises. This is becoming an increasingly frequent phenomenon due to climate change and armed conflict. Jeffrey Sachs (2012) has warned that many parts of the world will become "uninhabitable or at least uneconomic" as a result. Estimates of the impending number of refugees range from fifty million to one billion. Sachs points specifically to water (either too much or too little) as the main factor. This pertains not just to low-lying areas but also to semi-arid ones. It impacts greatly on human security and on the ultimate level of survival. Sachs points out that, for example, the violence in Darfur and in Somalia is caused by food and water insecurity.

However, borders are not necessarily open and Piguet et al. (2011) point out that mobility is strongly affected by political decisions. Forced migrants are typically thought of as the neediest because of meager material resources and being dispossessed. But it is likely at the outset they represent a broader cross-section of the population and thus have education and other skill levels closer to the average (McAdam 2011). Others pose the question of whether migration represents an example of adaptation or the failure to adapt.

Piguet et al. (2011) examined the governance framework in which migration flows take place. Those potentially forced to migrate as a result of climate change do not currently have official status as refugees. This issue is being hotly debated, where some argue that refugee status related to climate change would dilute the definition. This is in part due to a rigorous interpretation of the current concept of a refugee, but is not necessarily the best approach. It should also be noted that some oppose the extension of refugee status for fear of opening the floodgates due to migration. With respect to recent climate change treaties themselves, there has been slow progress on this issue (Hodgkinson et al. 2009). Refugee status matters greatly with respect to governments providing protection and assistance (Aminzadeh 2007; McAdam 2011). While these forms of assistance are strongly emphasized, there is inadequate attention to the role of resilience in assessing their need and effectiveness.

One of the features of climate change is that its slow onset could generate a new type of refugee, one with significant advanced time for planning. Advance plans are well intended but might be potentially rigid. There is a great opportunity to build in flexibility in various ways to increase resilience capacity when things do not go as planned. Another factor is that this migration is likely to take place in waves, so that social connections, especially with respect to kindred, are likely to be the key.

As to resilience strategies, in addition to providing resources, it is very important to provide training on how to best use them in the new environment. It is also important to gauge the length of stay and transition to temporary status, rather than just visitation. It is important to maintain communities and to prepare a population for advancement on the journey, including the return to their homeland. Even in places where there have been efforts to ease the plight of refugees for decades, concerns over human security continues (see, e.g., UNDP, 2013). Part of this is the dilemma of assistance, which can often turn into a dependency relationship.

6.4 Scale

In addition to applying resilience to several topic areas, this volume also addresses resilience at several levels or scales. The discussion has been implicit in many cases, but we provide a summary set of cross-references to the discussion at the following scale levels:

- Individual (households, businesses)
- Community (faith-based groups, refugees)
- Local area (markets, cities)
- Country (national economy)
- Region (confederations, water basins)
- Global (international economy)

In many cases one scale level is based on the aggregation of the next lowest scale level, which in turn is based on aggregations of still lower ones. For example, communities are composed of individuals, and the macroeconomy is composed of individual markets. Of course, in most cases the whole is greater than the sum of the parts. The analysis of resilience in the communities must include social psychology as well as individual psychology. In addition, the macroeconomy is composed to a great extent of aggregations of individual behavior that have tendencies of their own.

There is also a great deal of overlap between the scale levels. Markets don't have tidy geographic boundaries. Refugees spill over boundaries. Natural disasters definitely don't respect political boundaries. The matter of political boundaries is, however, especially important, since most responses to disasters require political actions and most major resilience initiatives require this as well. Yes, there are strong individual motivations, but large-scale mitigation projects (e.g., dams, levees, building codes, land use planning) require government action. Individual households and businesses can enhance resilience capacity. But again large scale efforts require political action in relation to emergency services (typically local level) warnings (typically regional level), and financial assistance for disaster recovery (state/province or national level).

Are there conflicts between scale levels? Most of the relationships are harmonious. The economy, even when not functioning perfectly, is typically in harmony. The hallmark of capitalism is that each individual household or business pursuing its own self-interest will act in a manner as to promote an overall efficient allocation of resources. This is also the intent of the few remaining planned economies. Of course, these individual motivations pertain to resilience as well. At the same time, the situation is not without its tensions and inequities, but these pertain more to issues within scale levels than across them. The major exception is when one region is being exploited by others. Individual communities are not always in harmony with higher strata, but this is the nature of things. For example, the Tiebout (1956) hypothesis is that people vote with their feet, meaning that they identify places to live that provide services they desire. This is, of course, the case with similar self-selection related to religion, political position, and sexual orientation.

This is not the place to discuss how to reduce all these tensions, but to focus on those relating to threats related to security from disasters and chronic problems. There are many examples of crises bringing disparate groups in communities, cities, or regions together. There are also many examples of assistance from the outside and typically higher levels. At the same time, there are examples of significant disharmonies, such as the intergovernmental bungling of the response to Hurricane Katrina or the military terrorizing the population of Darfur. Some of these can be addressed with advanced planning in relation to efforts to enhance resilience capacities. This advance planning provides opportunities for public participation, places policies out in the open, and affords an opportunity to be charitable. Of course, the situation can change in a crisis when the stark reality of serious resource scarcity sets in. Inventories, back-up equipment, shelter, medical care, etc. may not be efficiently or equitably allocated. It would help in this regard to institute explicit guidelines, continued public involvement, oversight, and stiff penalties for failure to perform these critical functions.

There are few real world examples of conflicts over resilience between scale levels, except for standard competition for resources. Revenues to pay for government services in general and various aspects of resilience in particular can be battlegrounds over who has access to a given tax base. Keeping the peace, or even dispensing assistance, often leads to a conflict between local police and provincial or national armed forces. Overall, public officials at all levels are quick to take credit for successes, and also quick to point fingers at other levels for failures.

References

Abadie A, Dermisi S (2011) World Trade Center tenant relocation patterns after September 11, 2001. Paper presented at the American Economic Association Annual Meetings, Denver

Aminzadeh S (2007) A moral imperative: the human rights implications of climate change. Hast Int Comparative Law Rev 30(2):231–265

Chang S, Rose A (2012) Economic recovery to disasters. Int J Mass Emerg Disasters 30(2):171–181

Chang S, Rose A, Johnson L (2011) What is national earthquake resilience? In: National earthquake resilience: research, implementation, and outreach. The National Academies Press, Washington, DC

Flynn S (2008) America the resilient: defying terrorism and mitigating natural disasters. Foreign Aff 87(2):2

Giesecke JA, Burns WJ, Barrett A, Bayrak E, Rose A, Slovic P, Suher M (2012) Assessment of the regional economic impacts of catastrophic events: CGE analysis of resource loss and behavioral effects of an RDD attack scenario. Risk Anal 32(4):583–600

Giesecke J, Burns W, Rose A, Barrett T, Griffith M (2015) Regional dynamics under adverse physical and behavioral shocks: the economic consequences of a chlorine terrorist attack in the Los Angeles financial district. In: Nijkamp P, Rose A, Kurtit K (eds) Regional science matters: studies dedicated to Walter Isard. Springer, Heidelberg

Hodgkinson D, Burton T, Young L, Anderson H (2009) Copenhagen, climate change 'refugees' and the need for a global agreement. Public Policy 4(2):155–174

Horwich G (1995) Economic lessons of the Kobe earthquake. Econ Dev Cult Chang 48(3):521–542

McAdam J (2011) Swimming against the tide: why a climate change displacement treaty is not the answer. Int J Refug Law 23(1):2–27

Petersen K, Rose A (2013) MSB/DHS program on community resilience: an overview.

Piguet E, Pecoud A, de Guchteneire P (2011) Migration and climate change: an overview. Refug Surv Q 30(3):1–23

Rose A (2004) Defining and measuring economic resilience to disasters. Disaster Prev Manag 13:307–314

Rose A (2009a) A framework for analyzing and estimating the total economic impacts of a terrorist attack and natural disaster. J Homeland Secur Emerg Manag 6(1):6

Rose A (2009b) Economic resilience to disasters. Community and Resilience Institute Research Report Number 8. ORNL

Rose A, Kustra T (2013) Economic considerations in designing emergency management institutions and policies for transboundary disasters. Public Manag Rev 15(3):446–464

Rose A, Oladosu G, Lee B, Beeler-Asay G (2009) The economic impacts of the 2001 terrorist attacks on the World Trade Center: a computable general equilibrium analysis. Peace Econ Peace Sci Public Policy 15(2):4

Sachs J (2012) Climate change refugees. Sci Am 306:43

Slovic P (1987) Perception of risk. Science 236(4799):280–285

Tiebout C (1956) A pure theory of local expenditures. J Polit Econ 64(5):416–424

United Nations Development Programme (UNDP) (2013) Human development Report 2013: the rise of the South: human progress in a diverse world. United Nations, New York

Valle L, Campanella T (2005) The resilient city: how modern cities recover from disaster. Oxford University Press, New York

Xie W, Rose A, Li S, He J, Li N, Ali T, Wei W (2016) Dynamic economic resilience and economic recovery from disasters: a quantitative assessment. Peking University, Beijing

Chapter 7
Empirical Analysis

7.1 Findings

Several studies have examined economic resilience empirically or with the use of simulation studies. The major pioneer is Tierney (1997), who surveyed businesses in the aftermath of the Northridge Earthquake and Midwest Floods. Rose and Lim (2002) translated Tierney's findings into specific measures of resilience of the Los Angeles electricity system. They identified such factors as time-of-day-use, electricity "importance," and production recapture as key to understanding why businesses that averaged an X % reduction of electricity were able to continue operation with much less than an X % reduction in their production goods and services. In fact, they found that these micro-level tactics resulted in a reduction of business interruption losses by more than 90 percent of baseline estimates, a reduction consistent with Tierneys' survey responses.

Rose and Liao (2005) also used the Tierney survey responses relating to water service disruptions to evaluate two major types of resilience: conservation of scarce inputs and enhanced ability to substitute other inputs for water. However overall, the above resilience strategies only yielded a reduction of losses by a few percentage points. In the Rose and Liao study, macro impacts follow from micro impacts of resilience through various type of general equilibrium effects (basically price and quantity multiplier effects). The macro impacts of resilience were double the micro-level impacts.

Other approaches to estimating resilience have been less evidence-based, but are still prominent in the literature. Several resilience factors have been incorporated into FEMA's loss estimation tool—HAZUS (FEMA 2013), which is being adapted for use in many other countries. The Direct Economic Loss Module (DELM) includes factors for individual businesses making up lost production at a later date by working overtime or extra shifts after their utility lifelines had been restored or after building damage had been repaired. These "recapture factors," developed by

A. Rose, *Defining and Measuring Economic Resilience from a Societal, Environmental and Security Perspective*, Integrated Disaster Risk Management, DOI 10.1007/978-981-10-1533-5_7

the author and Stephanie Chang, were based loosely on a synthesis of the literature, and the indication is that these factors are very high (ranging between 50 and 98 % for most sectors) for short periods. That is, customers are unlikely to cancel their orders for the output of disaster-sickened industries for short periods of time, because they have inventories on hand or long-standing supply-chain relationships. On the other hand, this type of resilience is likely to decline over time, and is likely to fall to zero after one year, if not after several months. The HAZUS Indirect Loss Module (IELM) includes such resilience factors as inventories, excess capacity, and the ability to increase imports and exports, also developed by Chang and Rose. However, there are no definitive estimates of the effectiveness of these resilience tactics for all cases, so it is necessary for the user to access primary or secondary data to specify their effectiveness.

Several simulation studies have been undertaken to estimate the effects of resilience on losses from disasters. Kajitani and Tatano (2009) used a survey to estimate the resilience of Japanese industries to various types of lifeline disruptions from disasters. Their findings represent the most definitive to date on a broad spectrum of resilience tactics. Rose et al. (2007a, b) estimated the resilience of the Los Angeles water and power systems to a 2-week outage due to a terrorist attack. They found that resilience could be as high as 90 %, primarily due to production recapture (see Sect. 8.3). Rose and Wei (2013) examined such resilience tactics as excess capacity, inventories, and export diversion to reduce potential losses from a 90-day shutdown of a major U.S. seaport complex. They found that the implementation of these resilience tactics could reduce GDP losses in the region by more than 70 %.

Note, however, these results should be carefully applied to natural disasters. In the case of terrorism, a specific infrastructure provider is targeted, but the rest of the economy is unscathed. Hence, when the water or power is restored, firms can resume production immediately. This is not necessarily the case for natural disasters, which inflict widespread damage, so that factories need to be repaired in addition to having their lifelines restored. Thus, the context needs to be factored into the potential effectiveness of some resilience tactics, such as production recapture, inventories or conservation, where the effectiveness of these tactics wanes over time (Rose 2007).

In addition the simulation studies cited above are biased to estimating resilience at its maximum effectiveness. This is not always the case due to the disarray accompanying most disasters, administrative obstacles, and personal failings. Moreover, Rose (2009) has pointed out that resilience can be eroded during large disasters as inventories are depleted, Draconian conservation becomes onerous, and opportunities for production recapture decline as customers abandon their traditional suppliers unable to deliver.

Two other factors impinge on effectiveness. The first is cost, but it turns out that resilience tactics are relatively inexpensive, especially compared to mitigation measures such as structural reinforcement of buildings or building of levees. Conservation more than pays for itself, input substitution requires a small penalty, the cost of inventories is just the carrying charge, emergency drills take relatively little time, production rescheduling involves the payment of overtime wages. Still even small costs can be serious obstacles in poor countries. Secondly, resilience may have negative side-effects. In the rush to rebuild, requests are often made to suspend environmental and safety regulations. Such requests must be carefully considered in light of the ancillary damages that could occur.

Overall, more case studies are needed to contrast successes (e.g., recovery from SuperStorm Sandy) and failures (e.g., recovery from Hurricane Katrina). Best practice examples can be very helpful, especially at the household level, where expertise is limited. Cross-cultural studies are enlightening as well in both broadening horizons and illustrating limits of resilient practices.

7.2 Resilience Indicators

Recently, interest has shifted to identifying individual resilience indicators or composites of them in the form of an overall index. Several well-intentioned examples include Cutter et al. (2010) and Sherrieb et al. (2010); as well as the excellent assessment by Cutter (2016). One major conclusion is that many of the components of resilience indicators to date are not in fact important to the resilience of individual businesses or the economy as a whole during the early stages of the recovery process. For example, the Index derived by Cutter et al. (2010) includes housing capital, equitable incomes, employment, business size, and position access. Subcomponent variables include percent employment, percent home ownership, business size, female labor force participation, and a proxy for single sector employment dependence. Hardly any of these indicators match those derived from a solid economic conceptual framework. Also, few have much to do with the operation of an individual firm or regional economy. Percent employment is a good initial measure of excess capacity in the labor force from which to draw; however, it does not take into account the fact that disasters are able to draw additional labor from neighboring communities either through market signals (higher wages) or for altruistic motivations. All of these criticisms apply to the creation and implementation of several more recent indicators (see, e.g., CARRI 2013; Cutter et al. 2014; ARUP and Rockefeller Foundation 2014).

Another approach to measuring and evaluating resilience is the establishment of a resilience threshold. This is analogous to the poverty threshold measured by incomes of $1.25/day per household. Some, for example, have proposed a resilience threshold of $5/day. This is, however, a narrow and limited approach. First, it appears arbitrary because there is no basis for the dollar value. Second it does not help much in relation to the destruction of major assets, such as houses or businesses. Here, a better measure would be asset holdings or access to credit or other financial assistance. Third, it is weak from a pure personal standpoint. Aspects of connectedness to social support groups (families, neighborhood associations, religious or social organizations) should be included. Also important is access to social services and to information about recovery alternatives. Lastly, one would ideally proceed beyond the minimum that this threshold indicator implies to a functional relationship that tracks the degree of resilience attained by higher levels of income or assets. It would be valuable to determine whether the indicator is characterized by increasing and then diminishing returns.

A major reason to construct a resilience index is not only to study the recovery process, but also to improve it. This speaks to the importance of *actionable variables*. Several indicators included in prior resilience indices refer to background conditions and general trends that can hardly be improved in the near-term aftermath. Moreover, improvement of some of them is not necessarily consistent with other economic goals. For example, diversification of the economy may come at the cost of some economic activity. Other indicators need to be acknowledged as very much being immutable during the key period in which businesses take resilient actions. Examples would include literacy rates, percent disabled, and percent minority population. More research is needed to replace these indicators with ones that really matter to economic resilience and that can be implemented in the short-run.

Finally, it is important to separately identify resilience tactics that are inherent in the survival mechanisms of businesses and households vs. those that require government policy assistance. This way future recovery efforts can better capitalize on existing capabilities and minimize duplication of government services. The focus of government can then be on facilitating this inherent resilience by removing obstacles to private enterprise, reducing wait times for assistance, and more effectively targeting its role in recovery.

Our analysis indicates that few resilience frameworks and no actual indices adequately focus on business operations in the aftermath of a disaster. We contend that business behavior, in relation to static and dynamic resilience, is the key to economic recovery, at least in the short-run. Thus, all prior attempts at developing a resilience index, while applicable and useful for long-run analyses (more than a year after the event), are less likely to be useful for the short-run.

Following Rose and Krausmann (2013), we outline the development of a short-run economic resilience index focusing on business behavior that is intended to help gauge recovery potential. The key issues are: (1) if and how to combine resilience actions at the micro, meso, and macro levels and (2) how to weight the various components. At the microeconomic level, i.e., the level of individual companies and organizations, a plethora of actionable measures to increase economic resilience exists. Business resilience consists of resilience options on both the customer and supplier side. While the former relates to coping with disaster impacts on the delivery of inputs and making effective use of resources, the latter pertains to ways to guarantee the delivery of outputs to customers. Some of these options relate to static economic resilience by aiming at diminishing losses (excess capacity, input or import substitution, etc.), while others facilitate speedy business recovery (reduce operating impediments, management, etc.) and hence belong to the dynamic resilience category.

The second consideration is how to evaluate the relative contribution of each resilience tactic (each measured as a single indicator). This issue of "weighting" has been finessed in nearly all prior cases. For instance, weights can be derived empirically, e.g., using surveys, or, as a fall back, from a theoretical model of the indicator to be measured. An alternative way to assign weights is by consensus or relevance with respect to specific policy initiatives. We propose that the best way to develop weights is based on evidence of the relative effectiveness of each type of resilience tactic. The weights would then have to be adjusted for differences in the context in which the index is to be applied, if it differs, and it likely will, from the original case. There is no one-size-fits-all approach to deriving weights and the method of choice will depend on the particular problem at hand. The reader is referred to Sect. 8.3 for more details on the compilation of a resilience index for business. The compilation for households would be analogous.

It is important to note that economics is only one part of the recovery from disasters. We are not suggesting economics is the only thing that matters in recovery from disasters, even just for economic recovery. In addition to the importance of non-economic factors, we also need to consider the existence of market failure, such as pollution, where the interests of business are not necessarily consistent with the interests of the community as a whole. In our context, this is exemplified by the possibility that the dispersal of toxic waste or ordinary pollutants might be accelerated by more rapid recovery, partly because environmental concerns may be given lower priority. One approach is to go beyond ordinary market-based economic indicators, such as gross domestic product (GDP), and utilize broader measures of economic well-being including the value of environmental resources and the value of household services. A major reason to construct a resilience index is not only to study the recovery process, but also to improve it. This speaks to the importance of *actionable variables*. Several indicators included in resilience indices refer to background conditions and general trends that can hardly be improved in the near-term aftermath. Moreover, improvement of some of them is not necessarily consistent with other economic goals. For example, diversification of the economy may come at the cost of some economic activity. This refers to the age-old tradeoff between risk and return, where diversification is a risk reduction strategy. However, this is not to suggest diversification is not a worthwhile consideration, but just that one need consider its downsides. Beyond that, some of the other indicators need to be acknowledged as very much being immutable during the key period in which business take resilient actions. Examples would include literacy rates, percent disabled, and percent minority population. More research is needed to replace these indicators with ones that can be implemented in the short-run.

Community resilience does of course require a broader set of indictors. Moreover, background conditions relating to human and community "wellness" are likely to be key, e.g., individuals that are healthy and better educated are more likely to be resilient. Just as human development is helped by resilience, human development helps individuals and communities become more resilient.

The major challenge is whether a single index can best reflect the features of resilience at various levels of the economic aggregation hierarchy. We suggest it is best to separate the three levels first, and then explore ways to combine them.

Table 7.1 Calculation steps for a resilience index

I. Basic calculations
A. Assessment
1. Identify resilience tactics (indicators) from guidelines and own assessment
2. Categories
a. Production (conservation, substitution, inventories, excess capacity)
b. Finance (retained earnings, credit rating)
c. Emergency response plan
d. Supply-chain considerations (critical inputs, back-ups)
e. Business logistics (location, transportation, infrastructure access)
f. Background conditions (health of economy, labor pool, excess office space, governance)
B. Measurement of potential resilience
1. Calculate each indicator (potential for loss reduction as percentage)
2. Calculate weights (relative potential)
a. Within categories
b. Across categories
C. Implementation adjustment of potential (scale-down)
1. Positive factors (experience, manageable enterprise)
2. Obstacles (inexperience, lack of control, cost)
D. Upgrade potential for future improvement (each indicator)
1. Each indicator
2. Each obstacle
E. Update (periodic)
1. Reassess indicators
2. Recalculate indicators
3. Recalculate weights
II. Calculations for differences in threats
A. Threat type
B. Threat severity (finite set to obtain distribution)
C. Customer resilience to electricity outages

7.3 Construction of a Resilience Index

Table 7.1 presents the steps in the construction of a Resilience Index (RI) for an individual business. In terms of an overview of the outline, the calculation of a resilience index for a business involves 5 basic steps:

- *Assessment* refers to identifying the broad range of tactics that can reduce business interruption losses following a disaster.
- *Measurement of Potential Resilience* refers to determining the maximum proportion of losses that can be reduced by each tactic.
- *Implementation Adjustment* refers to scaling down the potential to real world levels, taking into account impediments to putting resilience in place.

Table 7.2 Relative prominence of resilience adjustments for electric power outages in Los Angeles

Resilience factor	PE effect	GE effect
Adaptive electricity substitution	6.9	5.5
Electricity conservation	6.1	5.5
Electricity importance	28.7	15.1
Distributed generation	28.1	20.4
Production rescheduling	79.4	77.1
Total	89.6	86.0

Source: Rose et al. (2007a)

- *Upgrade* refers to finding ways to improve performance over time.
- *Update* is self-explanatory.

However, accurate measurements of resilience would differ for the type of threat (earthquake, hurricane, terrorist attack), as well as severity of the threat (to make this manageable one need only demarcate a few levels). So the RIs would have to be recalculated for each pairing of individual threat and severity to begin. Approaches to integrating and condensing all these calculations would facilitate this process.

Much of the data at the micro level would be known by each individual firm; major exceptions would be aspects of A2e and A2f. Other data sources would need to be accessed for the extension of the RI to the meso (market, sector) and macro (community, regional economy) levels. US Department of Commerce data and data from commercial sources, such as Dun and Bradstreet, would be prime candidates.

Examples of basic data for the calculation of RIs relating to resilience to electric power disruptions are summarized in Table 7.2 and are based on simulation studies by Rose et al. (2007a); Rose and Wei (2013). Studies by others based on actual experience or simulations could be used in a similar manner (see, e.g., Kajitani and Tatano 2009). The table identifies alternative tactics (indicators), and each numerical entry measures the percentage reduction in business interruption (BI) that each tactic can provide for either a water or power disruption, i.e., the estimate of resilience potential.

Several resilience tactics are available on the supplier-side (see, e.g., Lave et al. 2005). These include relatively expensive options, such as spare transformers, as well as less expensive options, such as expediting service restoration (basically dynamic economic resilience in the form of recovering more quickly).

On the customer-side, there are more widespread and less expensive options. Rose et al. (2007a) identify these resilience tactics and measure their effectiveness directly and indirectly (through upstream and downstream supply-chain effects) for a simulated terrorist attack of the Los Angeles electricity system. The usefulness of the study for our purposes is that it isolates the influence of outages themselves. Unlike an earthquake, which causes widespread destruction, an electricity system targeted by terrorists enables us to evaluate it alone. Of course, some of the implications of resilience in this context would then have to be modified for the case of an

Table 7.3 Resilience effectiveness indices for electric power outages

Resilience factor	PE effect		GE effect	
	Weights	Contribution	Weights	Contribution
Adaptive electricity substitution	4.6	4.1	4.4	3.8
Electricity conservation	4.1	3.6	4.4	3.8
Electricity importance	19.2	17.2	12.2	16.5
Distributed generation	18.8	16.8	16.5	14.2
Production rescheduling	53.2	47.7	62.4	53.7
Total	100.0	89.6	100.0	86.0

earthquake as discussed below. The basic findings by Rose et al. (2007a) are presented in Table 7.3. They pertain to the effects of changes in resilience through partial equilibrium (PE) effects, or the operation of a business (or household) entity itself, and general equilibrium (GE) effects, or the operation of the economy as a whole. The entries in the table represent the maximum potential percentage of BI losses that can be averted with the implementation of each resilience tactic.

Unlike other inputs, conservation of electricity is a very limited option. Rose et al. (2007a) estimate it to be 5 % based on a refinement of survey data by Tierney (1997). Increased (adaptive) interfuel substitution has the potential to reduce the elasticity of substitution between electricity and various fuels by 10 %, though this results in a significantly lower amount of resilience effectiveness.

Inventories (customer storage) is not a major option in the case of electricity. Electricity isolation differs by sector, ranging from levels of 70 % in various transportation-related sectors to 0 % in various manufacturing sectors (ATC 1991). Distributed generation, on-site alternatives to centralized electricity delivery, differ by location, but for the City of Los Angeles values ranged from 10 % in most sectors to 50 % in sectors with very large firms (e.g., Petroleum Refining), sensitive production processes (e.g., Semi-conductors), or where implementation is relatively easy (e.g., Security Brokers).

Production rescheduling also differs by sector, with very high rates for those sectors whose deliveries are not time-sensitive (e.g., Durable Manufacturing) and low rates for those whose are (e.g., Hotels and Restaurants) (Rose and Lim 2002; FEMA 2014). The analysis also assumed that a 2-week outage will not cause any permanent change in customer-supplier relationships.

Note that resilience is not additive across all tactics (indicators), as there is some overlap; hence total resilience is not the simple sum of the column entries in Table 7.3. Weights are obtained for each tactic/threat combo by dividing each entry (percentage reduction) in a column by the sum of column entries (not the "Total" at the bottom of the column of the table). The PE and GE Resilience Indices are presented in Table 7.3. Note that the first column of entries for each level of application represent the weight of each resilience tactic, while the second column represents the index if all were applied simultaneously. If an individual resilience tactic were to be applied in isolation, one would refer to the values in Table 7.2.

A reminder that the above simply measures resilience effectiveness, and that a full benefit-cost analysis cannot be undertaken until the analysis is extended to cost-effectiveness and the benefits side is estimated as well (see following chapter). Still, it is a valuable first step toward operationalizing the resilience concept and combining indicators into an overall index.

A production theory framework can provide guidelines for data collection in relation to formulating specific questions. First, the input variables in the production function give rise to an array resilience tactics, and can thus act as a checklist, as in Table 7.1. Second, questions can be posed in relation to the resilience metric discussed in Chap. 6: the percentage of potential losses averted by the implementation of each resilience tactic. The follow-on question would request information on the cost of implementation. The value of the lost production (i.e., sales revenue) would provide benefits information.

A cost effectiveness resilience index can be developed by first substituting units of effectiveness per dollar cost for each of the tactics in the above example. The remaining steps are exactly the same as those just explained.

References

Applied Technology Council (1991) ATC-25: seismic vulnerability and impact of disruption on lifelines in the conterminous United States. Federal Emergency Management Agency/Applied Technology Council, Redwood City

ARUP and Rockefeller Foundation (2014) City resilience framework. Ove ARUP & Partners International, London. https://assets.rockefellerfoundation.org/app/uploads/20150530121930/City-Resilience-Framework1.pdf

CARRI (2013) Building resilience in America's communities: observations and implications of the CRS pilots. Community and Regional Resilience Institute Report. http://www.resilientus.org/wp-content/uploads/2015/04/CRS-Final-Report.pdf

Cutter S (2016) The landscape of disaster resilience indicators in the USA. Nat Hazards 80:741–758

Cutter S, Burton CG, Emrich CT (2010) Disaster resilience indicators for benchmarking baseline conditions. J Homeland Secur Emerg Manag 7:51

Cutter S, Ash K, Emrich C (2014) The geographies of community disaster resilience. Glob Environ Chang 29:65–77

Federal Emergency Management Agency (FEMA) (2013) Multi-hazard loss estimation methodology (HAZUS®MH MR4). http://www.fema.gov/library/viewRecord.do?id=3726

Federal Emergency Management Agency (FEMA) (2014) Multi-hazard loss estimation methodology (HAZUS®MH MR4).

Kajitani Y, Tatano H (2009) Estimation of lifeline resilience factors based on empirical surveys of Japanese industries. Earthq Spectra 25(4):755–776

Lave L, Apt J, Morgan G (2005) A worst case electricity scenario: the benefits and costs of prevention. Paper presented at the Second Annual CREATE Symposium on the Economics of Terrorism. USC, Los Angeles

Rose A (2007) Economic resilience to natural and man-made disasters: multidisciplinary origins and contextual dimensions. Environ Hazards 7(4):383–395

Rose A (2009) Economic resilience to disasters. Community and Resilience Institute Research Report Number 8. ORNL

Rose A, Lim D (2002) Business interruption losses from natural hazards: conceptual and methodology issues in the case of the Northridge earthquake. Environ Hazards Hum Soc Dimens 4:1–14

Rose A, Liao S (2005) Modeling resilience to disasters: computable general equilibrium analysis of a water service disruption. J Reg Sci 45(1):75–112

Rose A, Krausmann E (2013) An economic framework for the development of a resilience index for business recovery. Int J Disaster Risk Reduct 5:73–83

Rose A, Wei D (2013) Estimating the economic consequences of a port shutdown: the special role of resilience. Econ Syst Res 25(2):212–232

Rose A, Oladosu G, Liao S (2007a) Business interruption impacts of a terrorist attack on the electric power system of Los Angeles: customer resilience to a total blackout. Risk Anal 27(3):513–531

Rose A, Oladosu G, Liao S (2007b) Regional economic impacts of a terrorist attack on the water system of Los Angeles: a computable general disequilibrium analysis. In: Richardson H, Gordon P, Moore J (eds) The economic costs and consequences of a terrorist attack. Edward Elgar Publishing Company, Cheltenham

Sherrieb K, Norris F, Galea S (2010) Measuring capacities for community resilience. Soc Indic Res 99:227–247

Tierney K (1997) Impacts of recent disasters on businesses: the 1993 Midwest floods and the 1994 Northridge earthquake. In: Jones B (ed) Economic consequences of earthquakes: preparing for the unexpected. National Center for Earthquake Engineering Research, Buffalo, pp. 189–222

Chapter 8
Risk Management

8.1 Cost-Effectiveness

To make prudent resource management decisions, one must consider the cost of each resilience tactic as well as its effectiveness. One tactic might be capable of reducing more than twice the BI losses of another, but if it costs ten times as much to implement, the former is not the better option.

We begin with a general overview of cost considerations. Most adaptive conservation more than pays for itself when it represents a productivity improvement, such as an increase in energy-efficiency (producing the same amount but with less energy). A more general definition of conservation (reducing the amount of an input irrespective of its effect on output) can incur net positive costs.[1] Input substitution requires a small penalty for using a less optimal input combination. Import substitution involves an increase in costs from utilizing higher-cost sources and/or increasing transportation distances. Relocation can be somewhat expensive if it involves a physical move; however, the increasing role of telecommunications, and the prospects for working in cyberspace and tele-commuting, have significantly decreased this cost. Emergency planning exercises take little time and incur relatively low costs. Production rescheduling involves the payment of overtime wages.

Some resilience tactics are primarily inherent, and simply await their utilization once the disaster strikes. The cost of inventories is just the carrying charge and not the value of the inventories themselves, which simply replace resources that would've been paid for otherwise. Excess capacity involves a similar cost, though some of this capacity is often planned in order to enhance business flexibility or to accommodate downtime for maintenance; these aspects should not be charged to disaster resilience. Production Isolation, instances where some production activities are separated from the need for one or more inputs, is inherent in the system, and

[1] Conservation often involves the installation of energy-saving equipment. When this more than pays for itself, an energy-efficiency improvement has taken place.

A. Rose, *Defining and Measuring Economic Resilience from a Societal, Environmental and Security Perspective*, Integrated Disaster Risk Management,
DOI 10.1007/978-981-10-1533-5_8

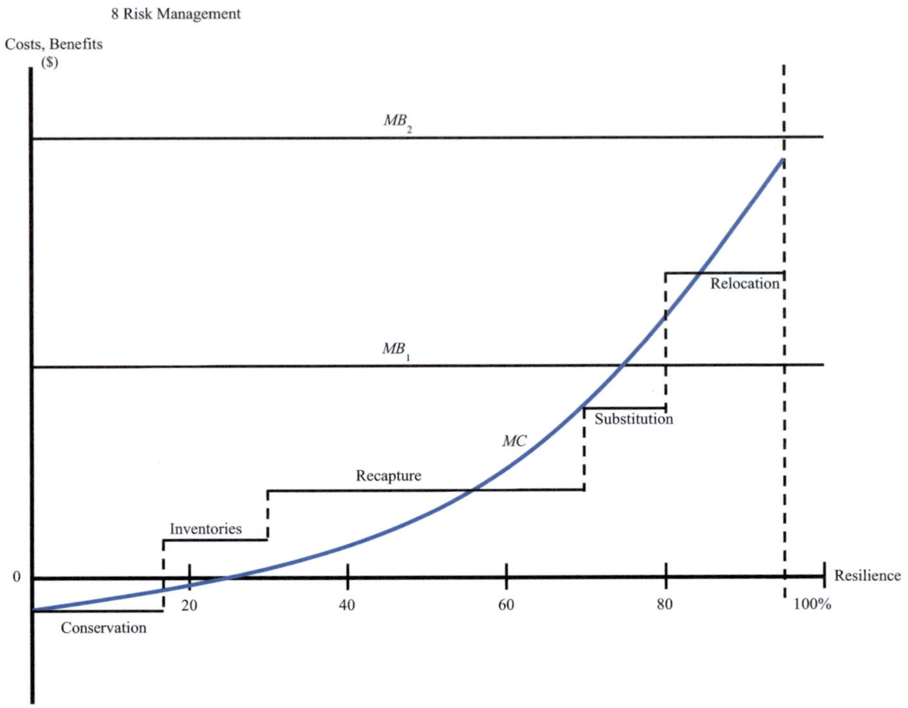

Fig. 8.1 Benefit-Cost Analysis of Resilience

should likewise not be charged to resilience unless it is expressly done for that purpose.

Once the cost per unit of effectiveness, expressed in percentage terms or in terms of dollars of net revenue from business interruption loss prevention, is determined the options should be ranked from lowest cost to highest, as depicted in the stylized example in Fig. 8.1. The result is the increasing marginal cost curves (a step-function thus far); this limit would be the maximum percentage or dollar amount of resilience possible. Note that since most conservation more than pays for itself, the function begins in the negative cost range.

The cost of each resilience tactic is affected by the context in which it is implemented. First, for any given tactic, its cost is not likely to be constant over the range of application (effectiveness). Nearly all economic processes eventually exhibit diminishing returns, resulting in a marginal cost curve (or step-function for now) that increases at an increasing rate, as in Fig. 8.1. For example, there might be several conservation options, likely with different costs. Import substitution would be another example, where increasing amounts would need to be brought in from longer distances, or even higher cost suppliers at the same distance. Diminishing returns are also likely applicable in the cases of relocation and technological change. This consideration provides a rationale for fitting a curve through the step function as is done in Fig. 8.1. Note also that the total cost of achieving any target level of resilience is reflected by the area under the marginal cost (MC) curve; it represents the mathematical integration of the first-derivative (marginal term) to yield the total.

The context in which the disaster strikes and resilience is implemented also has an influence on the effectiveness side. Relevant factors include the disaster type, magnitude, and recovery duration, as well as background conditions relating to the economy, such as its economic health at the time of the disaster and its geographic location. For example, inventories are finite and more likely to run out in disasters for which the duration of recovery is long. Production recapture also erodes over time, as customers begin to seek other suppliers. Excess capacity is dependent on the business cycle (e.g., one reason that relocation was so effective after the World Trade Center attacks was because New York City was in the throes of a recession, which then provided a great deal of vacant office and manufacturing space).

8.2 Benefit-Cost Analysis

Resilience can be couched in a benefit-cost analysis (BCA) framework by bringing its rewards formally into the picture. For purposes of simplification, we can think of the benefits as the net revenue of business interruption losses avoided. At first this might best be represented by a horizontal marginal benefit (MB) curve, reflecting equal additional increments of benefits for each percentage increase in resilience. For example, if potential BI losses are $1,000,000 in net revenue terms, then each percentage of resilience has a marginal benefit of $10,000. In this case, the marginal benefit function is constant by definition.[2] If the horizontal axis of Fig. 8.1 were measured in terms of physical units of production, then it could be non-linear. The optimal level of resilience would be at the point at which the marginal cost and marginal benefit curve intersect.[3] Even without a precise numerical example, we can draw some insights from Fig. 8.1. All cost-saving resilience options would be taken, because they yield guaranteed net benefits. Also, given the relatively low cost of many of the tactics, at least in some of their initial applications, it is likely that a fairly high level of resilience would be chosen.

---

[2] For example, economies of scale would actually increase the marginal benefits successively as resilience is carried out, counter to the more standard downward-sloping marginal benefit curve. Net revenue would also increase if fixed costs are significant. Working in the opposite direction, however, would be factors such as keeping the business open at some minimum level for the sake of its public image. The most significant factor affecting the MB curve, however, would be on the gross revenue side. The perfectly competitive firm could sell as much of its product as needed at a constant price to maximize profits, which is essentially at a constant marginal revenue. However, firms in imperfectly competitive markets would face a declining marginal revenue curve, putting pressure on the net revenue function to decline as well.

[3] This condition holds even for an increasing marginal benefit curve, as long as its slope is flatter than the marginal cost curve.

We note additional considerations relating to important characteristics of resilience tactics. One pertains to whether a given tactic yields benefits only to an individual business or whether these benefits apply more broadly. Nearly all of the micro-level resilience tactics that we have discussed thus far, with a focus on the customer-side, have limited spillover effects. However, the opposite is true for resilience tactics on the supplier-side. An example is that of redundancy, such as the presence of a back-up water pipeline system. In this case, the benefits are not simply limited to maintaining revenue to the supplier, but to avoid business interruption for all its customers. Thus, while redundant systems are relatively much more expensive than the resilience options just discussed, their benefits are much more widespread. In fact, they basically exhibit something akin to "public goods" benefits.

A further consideration needs to be taken into account on the cost side for redundant systems, as well as some demand-side tactics, such as inventories or back-up equipment. Rose (2009) and others make the case that customer-side resilience tactics need not be implemented until the disaster strikes, which would appear to give them a cost advantage over mitigation and supplier-side tactics such as redundancy. However, most forms of inherent resilience, such as inventories and back-up, are in place whether or not the disaster strikes. While they lack the flexibility that other customer-side tactics have, there is a positive ramification of this—they exist to protect against *many* threats over the course of their lifetime. Thus, their cost-effectiveness is much higher than if one considers only a single threat. The MB function in our analysis can readily be adjusted for these features by incorporating all of these benefits of implementing the given resilience tactic and also considering a distribution of threats for which it reduces BI losses. Thus, the larger the number of customers the water utility with a redundant system serves, the greater its benefits, and the more threats a stockpile protects against, the greater its benefits.

We illustrate these points in relation to a tactic such as redundancy in Fig. 8.1. The MB curve we have been discussing thus far ($MB_{1)}$ would be raised significantly if we took into account that it protects against a distribution of threats (see, e.g., $MB_{2)}$. On the other hand, we would have to multiply the benefits by the probability of their occurrence, which would put downward pressure on the MB curve. In the vast majority of cases, the net effect would be a lower MB curve because the probabilities of extreme events are so low.

Also, the fact that benefits of a redundant system accrue beyond simply the electric or water utility providing the service and extend to all of their customers would significantly increase the overall benefits. Implicitly, the MB curve has been defined thus far in terms of the rewards to the entity implementing this resilience tactic—the electric or water utility. However, the gains to all the customers are likely to be much greater; in essence, these gains would be the net revenue losses prevented by this resilience tactic, and thus likely to be at least an order of magnitude larger than the benefits to the utility itself.[4] The latter essentially represents a type of social benefit of implementing the resilience tactic. This is what is illustrated by MB_2 in Fig. 8.1, which is significantly higher than MB_1, though not necessarily drawn to scale.[5] One further ramification of this situation is the difference between the private optimum and social optimum, as well as the associated motivations. The utility's decision to implement this resilience tactic would be based on its own private marginal benefits, while, from the standpoint of society, it would be best to implement a higher level (the classic "public goods" optimal resource allocation problem). This raises public policy issues related to how to induce behavior consistent with the best interests of society as a whole. The desired outcome is likely to be achieved more readily in the cases of government-owned or -run utilities. For investor-owned utilities, subsidies or some form of regulation would be required.

The reader is referred to Rose (2016) for empirical estimates of benefit-cost ratios for resilience tactics in the electric utility example presented in the previous chapter. The analysis discusses several of the complications that must be addressed in the estimation process.

References

Rose A (2009) Economic resilience to disasters. Community and Resilience Institute Research Report Number 8. ORNL

Rose A (2016) Benefit-cost analysis of economic resilience actions. In: Cutter C, S (ed) Oxford research encyclopedia of natural hazard science. Oxford University Press, New York, forthcoming

[4] The order-of-magnitude estimate stems from a simple back-of-the-envelope calculation. Electricity and water inputs represent less than 5 % each on average of total production costs of nearly all businesses in the economy. Assuming, rates of return (or profit rates in general) are reasonably equal across all business enterprises, again on average, this means that net revenue losses are more than 20 times higher for the economy than for the utility supplier. Moreover, this number increases when indirect (multiplier or general equilibrium) effects are taken into account.

[5] Strictly speaking only resilience tactics that have this characteristic (mainly supply-side ones) would have their MB segments raised. This would make for a likely non-monotonically increasing or decreasing MB curve and would complicate the identification of an optimum.

Chapter 9
Co-benefits

Cutter (2016; p. 742) has recently stated "it is the need for making the business case for investments in risk reduction and resilience which is driving the policy agendas articulated in the Sendai Frameworks for Disaster Loss Reduction."[1] There is no doubt that the primary motivation of businesses is to maximize profits. On the surface, only those disaster risk management (DRM) actions, which include both (pre-disaster) mitigation and (post-disaster) resilience, that are viewed as promoting this objective will be undertaken, though not all of these actions are recognized. But there are several broader benefits of DRM to businesses themselves and to the economy as a whole that are typically neglected, and hence businesses underinvest in DRM both from their own perspective and also from the standpoint of society.

We refer to the broader benefits, or spillover effects, of DRM as *Co-Benefits*. When a business installs a sprinkler system to protect against fire spreading on its premises, it also helps protect adjacent buildings and an entire community. This is also the case for strengthening the foundation of a tall building, lest it collapse on its neighbors, or for instituting better water drainage practices that reduce flooding potential for the community. It also applies to accelerating business recovery, which puts people back to work and provides needed inputs to other businesses in the affected area. More broadly actions by any one business can contribute to overall community well-being in terms of improving the quality of life and promoting economic growth and stability. These Co-Benefits are not all captured by the firm that pays for them, and this leads to underinvestment in DRM.

Overall, private sector DRM strategies have many benefits, including avoided losses and other direct or indirect benefits for the firms implementing them, as well as positive spillover effects ("externalities") for other firms, the macroeconomy, and society as a whole. However, businesses tend not to engage in DRM sufficiently from a societal perspective, because of internal decision-making limitations and because they cannot capture many of these spillovers benefits. Therefore, greater

[1] Cutter also suggests that this is driving the interest in resilience indicators.

A. Rose, *Defining and Measuring Economic Resilience from a Societal, Environmental and Security Perspective*, Integrated Disaster Risk Management,
DOI 10.1007/978-981-10-1533-5_9

awareness of Co-Benefits and government and NGO incentives are needed to encourage private firms to increase investment in DRM (see Rose 2016).

Another source of Co-Benefits pertains to broader gains to society apart from disasters. This refers to DRM investments that benefit disadvantaged segments of the population and that contribute to sustainable development itself, such as vaccinating their employees or using more durable materials in their buildings. Many of these gains are external to the firm but feed back positively onto businesses themselves by promoting economic stability, spawning a healthier and more productive workforce, etc.

Still another category of Co-Benefits can be captured primarily by businesses themselves, if they are able to recognize them. These include DRM investments that improve the image of the firm or that otherwise lead to an increase in long-run profits, such as actions that are viewed as being in the public interest or that protect society from catastrophic risk. Ironically, many of these Co-Benefits are more tangible and immediate than most ordinary DRM benefits, which may not appear until a disaster has struck many years after the investment has been made.

Inducements are often needed for businesses to invest in a manner and at a level that captures these Co-Benefits for themselves and/or their host economies. Examples include providing businesses with better information on how they can reap some of the rewards of broader Co-Benefits, developing more versatile financial instruments, or providing them with subsidies that correspond to some portion of the Co-Benefits that contribute to societal goals. Although the subsidies represent a cost to government, it may be less expensive, as well as more effective, to have the private sector undertake these efforts. The appropriate design of incentives, preferably based on strong theoretical foundations and empirical evidence, is critical to cost-effective implementation of DRM.

This chapter analyzes many important facets of private sector investment in DRM, primarily from an economic perspective. It is intended as a first step to greater investment in DRM by identifying potential Co-Benefits, explaining why they are not always pursued, and suggesting ways to integrate them into private sector decision-making.

9.1 Integration into Business Culture and Sustainability Planning

The infrequency and sporadic nature of disasters cause a serious perception problem with respect to DRM. Learning is possible, but limited by institutional memory. Often mitigation and resilience are viewed as areas of concern separate from day-to-day business activity.

Several analysts have suggested, however, that it is prudent for businesses to integrate DRM into their general business strategies and practices. Essentially, this is a general way of capturing some Co-Benefits. For example, Zolli and Healy

(2012) have emphasized the importance of organizational and operational flexibility, which makes businesses more capable of coping with drastic change. Sheffi (2005) has provided numerous examples of supply-chain rigidity that led to business failure in the aftermath of a disaster, but is now countered by a broader view of the supply chain as a web that includes back-up sources.

In addition, in many countries a business-continuity industry has been spawned to meet the increasingly needed functions that more companies are realizing are beyond their own expertise or can be applied more cheaply if contracted out (e.g., information technology back-up, massive clean-up, logistical support, relocation). Large companies in industrialized countries can readily form and staff their own emergency management office, but smaller firms and firms in developing countries are less likely to be able to do so. The professionalization of DRM at the operations level in this new service industry fills a much-needed gap.

Resilience is considered to be the response to short-run shocks, while sustainability refers to maintaining a long-run development path in which actions by the current generation do not compromise the well-being of future generations, with an emphasis on maintaining the value of natural capital and human capital, not just physical capital. If a country cannot survive short-run shocks, it clearly will not be sustainable. One other aspect of the relationship is key: transforming the ingenuity that arises from short-run resilience into longer-term practices to promote sustainability. Rose (2014) has specified the following steps that can help achieve this goal:

- Identify effective resilience tactics at the micro (business), meso (industry/market), and macro (regional/national) levels based on actual experience. For example, ingenuity in conserving and substituting for critical resources under extreme stress should be examined for their more permanent potential under normal conditions.
- Develop resilience indicators based on evidence of successful practices to monitor progress on resilience capacity. Even though disasters may be sporadic, the need to develop ways to mute their negative impacts should be a continuous process.
- Disseminate findings on best-practice resilience tactics and community response. Likewise, the continuous dissemination of information about resilience will help make it ingrained in daily life.
- Evaluate the cost-effectiveness of resilience. This helps ensure resilience will be implemented as efficiently as possible, thereby helping to remain on or return to a sustainable path.
- Analyze the strategic tradeoffs between mitigation and resilience in terms of cost-effectiveness. Resilience should not be assessed in isolation of other major strategies, and that assessment should be done in terms of their ability to cope with short-run crises and to contribute to long-run sustainability.
- Identify ways to make resilience in the face of crises enduring, so as not to repeat previous mistakes. A good institutional memory contributes to both resilience and sustainability.

- Identify ways to transform short-run resilience responses into sustainability strategies. The view of resilience should go beyond consideration of individual tactics and should be evaluated in terms of broader community strategies that capture synergies.
- Steer the economy and related systems to greater flexibility in terms of resource provision and utilization. A key attribute of resilience is flexibility, and ways need to be found to take advantage of this attribute, as in broadening the array of sustainable future paths.

Overall, the many Co-Benefits of DRM represent a type of "Resilience Dividend." This concept heightens the potential of DRM to not only reduce disaster losses but also to enhance the prospects for future growth and development, and hence sustainability. It is part of what is now known as the "Triple Dividend of Resilience", where resilience is defined more broadly than in most of this volume (Tanner et al. 2015; Surminski and Tanner 2016). In addition to contributing directly to reducing vulnerability to disasters, resilience reduces uncertainties that promote entrepreneurship and investment, and also provides tangible joint product benefits other than those related to reducing risk.

9.2 Shortfalls in Private Sector Investment in DRM

9.2.1 Private Sector Investment Decisions

The primary objective of businesses is to maximize profits, and for many firms the focus is only on the short term. Secondary objectives, such as increasing market share, are usually consistent with this primary concern as well, but are more long term. DRM will be undertaken by businesses as long as it is consistent with profit maximization. Most DRM initiatives involve investment, so the objective is often couched in terms of maximizing net present value or the internal rate of return. The latter principle is often used to compare or rank alternatives. Brugmann (2012) emphasizes the importance of factoring mitigation, adaptation and resilience into the picture, as opportunities to improve investment performance. He notes that this can help establish a market basis for DRM.

Investments have two interrelated features that other business activities do not have, or have to a lesser degree. First, the returns to the firm take place over the course of time. Second, because they take place in the future, the returns involve a degree of uncertainty. Interest rates are used to account for both features. Revenues in the future year are not directly comparable to each other, so the market interest rate is used to discount future returns to account for the time value of money. The interest rate is also used to adjust for risk, such that higher than market rates reflect a *risk premium*. Investments in new or unproven technologies are relatively more uncertain than others; these are characteristic of many of the larger DRM investments, which have to be customized. Another factor that translates into greater uncertainty surrounds the benefits of DRM. These benefits are the avoidance of lost profits, adjusted by the probability of occurrence of the disaster. These probabilities are highly uncertain, so the risk premium may be increased accordingly.

A major debate revolves around whether uncertainty reduces or merely postpones business investment. Doh and Pearce (2004) suggest that a context of continuous vs. discontinuous uncertainty makes a difference, with disasters clearly being in the latter category. A great deal of literature relates to regulatory uncertainty, which is also very applicable to disaster mitigation (e.g., building codes, zoning ordinances). Findings are mixed, however, on whether uncertainty inhibits forward movement (cf. Yang et al. 2004; Aragón-Correa and Sharma 2003). Carrera et al. (2003) and others note ways of capitalizing on uncertainty, such as the advantages of being a "first-mover" (another type of Co-Benefit). Hoffmann et al. (2009) provide an example of three factors in a case study of German electric utilities facing climate change regulation as influencing forward progress on investment: (1) securing competitive resources, (2) leveraging complementary resources, and (3) alleviating institutional pressure.

9.2.2 Private Sector Investment and the Public Sector

Although businesses continuously voice their support of free markets and opposition to government interference, most firms will work in a cooperative spirit if it is in their best interest. For enlightened business managers, best interest means not just short-run maximization of profits, but also maintenance of the business's image. Both of these factors augur well for businesses cooperating in sustainable development efforts.

Governments have led the charge to "mainstream" DRM into development planning, as exemplified by a case study of Jamaica (ODI 2014). That country has included a broad range of sectors and vulnerabilities into the plan, including transportation infrastructure, food security, ordinary flood protection, landslide risk reduction, and climate change. A Senegal case study (ODI 2014) indicates a very broad approach in which the country's National Platform brings together all ministries. At the same time, this study notes shortcomings, including a lack of coherence among levels of government and an absence of the requirement of environmental impact assessments prior to the undertaking of major projects.

Public sector investment decisions are not dissimilar to the private sector at the core. Benefit-cost analysis (BCA) is typically applied with the objective of maximizing the net present value of future returns. Given the uncertain nature of disasters, the benefit side of the ledger is often weighted by the probability of occurrence. In such an expected value setting, Co-Benefits for extreme events can readily exceed Direct Benefits of DRM because the weights are so low (the events are so infrequent). It should be kept in mind, however, that with regard to other decision criteria, such as minimizing regret, the probabilities do not come into play, and the avoidance of disaster is the key factor.

Two major differences between public and private sector decision criteria should be noted, however. First, public sector evaluations are usually required to consider all benefits to society, not just narrow benefits to a private enterprise, which are often confined to market values translated into revenues. In other words, at least in theory, government investment decisions should incorporate all Co-Benefits. Second, the government discount rate is usually considered to be lower than the private one for several reasons, including government's much greater resources that do not necessitate borrowing in capital markets and government's relative greater ability to absorb adverse shocks from uncertainty.

9.2.3 Private Sector Co-benefits

The major benefits to a firm from a DRM investment are the revenue losses avoided and any ancillary revenues it may receive. The latter would be exemplified by Co-Benefits in the form of salable by-products or joint products, such as a decision to install solar panels to insulate the firm against disruptions from central power stations, where excess solar electricity can be sold back to the grid. This is still a relatively short-sighted perspective, and its limitations are discussed both from the vantage point of the firm and society as a whole in the following sub-sections.

A more enlightened view of the firm's objectives incorporates longer-run considerations relating to its good name or its survival. DRM often provides broader social benefits that might be considered by the firm, as pressures from shareholders, incentive systems, etc., tend to focus private companies on the bottom line. Examples would be voluntary reductions in pollution that improve the firm's image and implementation of flood control practices that benefit the entire flood plain.

An in-depth discussion of Co-Benefits is presented elsewhere in this volume, so we confine ourselves to a brief summary list here without any detailed description. There are four major categories of Co-Benefits for which we provide some examples:

- *Benefits to the business undertaking the investments*
  - improved business image (from being a "good citizen")
  - improved credit rating (from increased stability)
  - improved ability to deal with multiple hazards (from business continuity planning)
- *Benefits to other businesses in the supply chain or geographic vicinity*
  - increased supply-chain stability (from business continuity)
  - reduction in contagion effects (from lower likelihood of fire spreading or falling debris)

- *Benefits to the general business climate*
  - reduced uncertainty (through lowering the likelihood- of disaster losses)
  - increased economic stability (from business continuity)
  - increased economic growth (from business continuity)
  - contributions to technological progress (from embodied technological improvements)
- *Benefits to society*
  - improved health and education (from employee-related measures)
  - improved environment (from more prudent use of resources)

9.2.4 Bounded Rationality

Economics has long been criticized for invoking simplifying assumptions about behavior, such as the profit maximization motive of businesses. A broader perspective has evolved that incorporates behavioral considerations. The main body of this approach is known as *bounded rationality*, and it focuses on various limitations to decision-making (see, e.g., Gigerenzer and Selten 2002). A classic example is myopia, which refers to the use of unduly short time horizons. The manager may only be interested in near-term gains, as opposed to long-term ownership considerations. Kuneuther et al. (2013) found that analogous myopia was the major deterrent in undertaking DRM by households in hazard-prone areas. Even major information campaigns to raise awareness have been relatively unsuccessful (Kunreuther 2006). A related phenomenon that also leads to market failure is that of asymmetric information. One key example is the "principal-agent" problem, best exemplified at the business level when the manager is not the owner. The manager's incentives may be end-of-year bonuses, often based on maximizing sales, rather than maximizing profits, which is more in line with the efficient allocation of resources.

These instances are pertinent to DRM decisions. A manager may see a mitigation measure as reducing profits in the year in which they are made, without considering the longer-term view that it will reduce disaster losses in the future. Myopia and split incentives are likely to lead to even less attention to broader societal benefits of DRM, such as poverty alleviation, economic stability, and sustainable growth. Thus, just demonstrating the existence of these broader Co-Benefits is not necessarily enough to achieve the desired action. Some remedies that would help promote the pursuit of Co-Benefits, but not necessarily in capturing them all, include working with owners rather than managers, appealing to the reputation of the firm, and giving priority for disaster assistance to those firms that cooperate in DRM.

Another limitation of decision-making is lack of information and the inability to process the information available. This concept extends to expertise as well. Yoshida and Deyle (2005) found access to expertise (primarily from engineers, insurance managers and consultants) to be the major determinant of small business investment in hazard mitigation. The emergence of the business continuity industry should help in this regard, especially for smaller firms who lack in-house expertise. This is even truer for home-owners, but programs like the Institute for Business and Home Safety (IBHS 2015) FORTIFIED Program in the U.S., which links expertise with higher standards, offers a promising approach.

The concept of *moral hazard* refers to engaging in negligent actions because the entity need not bear their full cost. The very nature of large businesses lends itself to this problem, as decisions by one person in the firm are not immediately, or even eventually, penalized. Many corporations are so large that accountability loses transparency or else is dissipated. All but the top officials are insulated from the other operations. It is the mid-level management that must voice concerns about disasters, but may be hesitant to do so, lest DRM expenditures come out of their own budgets. Moral hazard also arises for large firms when their negligent actions are forgiven by governments who lack influence over them.

9.3 Co-benefits of Public Sector Investment

9.3.1 Co-benefits to Society

Not adequately considering co-benefits of DRM is a major reason for underinvestment (Vorhies 2012). Public officials in general need to be better informed of these co-benefits and need to do a better job of communicating them to their finance ministries and to the business community.

To expand on the discussion in the previous section, there are several reasons why even the knowledge of Co-Benefits may not be sufficient for adequate public sector action. Such reasons come under the heading of "government failure", the counterpart to "market failure". One of them is the short time-horizon of elected officials, who often cannot see beyond the next election. A counterpart is the insulation of appointed officials. Further exacerbating the problem is the opportunity cost of DRM investment in relation to other goods and services that public officials may prefer to provide, as they view the public interest or their own political self-interest (Vorhies 2012). There are several ways of overcoming this problem. For example greater public participation in the decision process injects a two-way flow of information that promotes DRM. Flores and Smith (2010) have noted that democratic societies tend to do a better job in terms of DRM.

Government agencies are likely to improve access to funds through better communication. Templates for information-sharing, such as those developed by the U.S. Federal Emergency Management Agency (FEMA 2013), are one valuable model. Still, just a listing of the relevant co-benefits is only an easy first step. The next and much more difficult step is actually measuring them. Kousky (2012) and Vorhies (2012) provide examples relating to the evaluation of mitigation measures for housing in the form of retrofits, but note difficulties in implementation such as whether to value buildings according to market prices or replacement costs.

Some of the co-benefits are especially difficult to measure, as in assessing potential improvements to the business environment or to more general economic stability. It has not even been demonstrated yet that foreign direct investment (FDI) is driven in any major way by DRM. Many of the indirect standard effects of DRM, such as multipliers stemming from economic interdependence, can be measured by conventional models, such as input-output (I-O) and computable general equilibrium (CGE) models (see, e.g., Hallegatte 2008; Rose 2015). Externalities, or spillover effects, can be measured as well. For example, Rose et al. (2014) measured the side-effects of anti-terrorism measures such as traffic stops, bag and parcel checks, and closed-circuit television monitors. While the latter generated some loss of privacy, it also increased the feeling of security, which translates into increased commercial activity and more broadly an improved business climate to attract investment.

Another difficulty is in catering to various stakeholders. Not all of them are equally impacted, so distributional information is especially important. In addition, one must overcome the apparent bias of DRM with respect to higher income groups. Since they have much more at stake, they are likely to reap the greater share of absolute gains, though the relative position of lower income classes is relevant here, and DRM has the ability to prevent further deterioration of their material status.

9.3.2 Co-benefits to the Private Sector

Despite exponentially increasing financial losses from disasters, business spending on DRM has not kept pace. The issue is how to engage the private sector in DRM from a finance and implementation standpoint. Also important is how this engagement would influence government development planning.

One more direct and apparent benefit to the private sector relates to risk-taking. Analysts have long noted its important role in entrepreneurship, and it should not be stifled but rather enhanced. Investors work in the context of background risk not under their control, but disasters exacerbate this and can lead to greater risk aversion, which has a dampening effect on the entrepreneurial spirit. Reducing this background risk and providing better information on residual risk can help promote DRM. It leads to a context of "risk-conscious decision-making" (Hallegatte 2016, Ch. 2)

There is an important role for insurance in DRM. Insurance is provided by the private sector throughout most of the industrialized world, and its expansion into the developing world would be valuable for this purpose. However, these initiatives are likely to require backing through re-insurance, government subsidies, or government regulation (e.g., ceilings on liability/payouts). One of the especially beneficial aspects of insurance, when structured properly, is the inducement for mitigation.

This harkens back to fire loss coverage, where the insured were given reductions in premiums if they undertook sounder fire prevention practices. Lower insurance rates represent an additional co-benefit of DRM, in that it makes insurance more affordable to a larger number of people.

One of the key issues is being able to communicate effectively with businesses, taxpayers, and political supporters of these Co-Benefits. The main challenges are interrelated:

- Absence of controlled experiments that are the standard in the science fields but not possible in the disaster field, hence rendering analyses relatively more tenuous.
- Measuring and tracking investment effects is difficult, because first a baseline must be established and then the effects of investing ascertained (again difficult where controlled experiments are not possible, or impossible if the disaster does not strike)
- Having to do the measurement and communication in the context of uncertainty makes them relatively more difficult to come across as convincing and more difficult to understand by non-scientists.

9.4 Resilience Dividend as a Sustainable Development Theme

Awareness of Co-Benefits of DRM must be raised. Because so many of them are not part of individual business enterprise calculations, they are likely to be ignored. Also, because many of them are especially difficult to measure, their full contributions might not be fully appreciated. Knowledge transfer can be especially valuable in making the business case for DRM. Best-practice methods of evaluation, instruments for finance, and techniques for implementation can be very valuable in this regard. This should also be extended to what is referred to as "Next Practices," which are more forward looking and help developing countries overcome some of the mistakes and limitations of the past by learning from industrialized country experiences.

This study is only a first step in the process of improving the perceptions of the broad range of benefits of DRM. Below, we discuss some of the broader contributions of DRM in terms of a resilience "dividend."

9.4.1 No Regrets Strategy

One of the major features of the Co-Benefits approach to evaluating DRM investments is that many are not dependent on actually experiencing the disasters that they seek to prevent. Sometimes, such investments would be viewed as wasteful, but this is an unfair characterization, since from a probabilistic standpoint they are prudent. Thus, while the expected value of benefits (losses averted) are positive, the actual direct benefits may be viewed as zero. However, the Co-Benefits often take place irrespective of the occurrence of any disasters. It has been popular to refer to such instances as a "no-regrets" strategy, in that it reaps benefits irrespective of future outcomes. This terminology has come into widespread use in the climate change area, where tactics such as energy efficiency (reductions in energy use that more than pay for themselves) are considered meritorious on their own even if predictions about climate change are not accurate (IPCC 2014).

Clearly, pure no-regrets strategies are just a subset of DRM investments where Co-Benefits themselves outpace the costs. As such, they relieve the pressure on some highly visible projects that do not otherwise appear to have been needed. We should, however, not let the perfect be the enemy of the good, in that investments with partial offsets of costs through Co-Benefits are worth seeking on a probabilistic basis.

9.4.2 Shared Growth and Social Benefits

Prudent DRM investments will increase not only the profit margins of firms but also benefit the entire economy directly and indirectly. Direct benefits stem from the increased capital stock and production (contributions to a higher GDP) of the firm itself. Indirect effects, or Co-Benefits, stem from the many categories discussed in this chapter, including multiplier effects, employment opportunities and tax revenues in all cases, and environmental and broader social benefits in some cases. Moreover, the reduction of uncertainty can have a stimulating effect on both the firm and the overall economy through many conduits including attracting more foreign direct investment.

Most of the population can share the gains of economic growth. Increased employment helps reduce poverty and provides improved health care for those employed (again directly and indirectly). Increased tax revenues can be used to help others, not only in terms of health care, but also education and other social services. Reduced uncertainty provides broader social benefits as well in terms of locational choices, personal investment planning, and human resilience.

There is some controversy about which socioeconomic groups benefit most from DRM. The well-to-do benefit because they have the most assets. On the other hand, the poor often live in areas with greater hazard exposure and vulnerability. Moreover, because they live on the edge of subsistence, even relatively smaller losses can be relatively more injurious to them. Economic and social equity implications of DRM need to be examined and refinements made where they violate a society's principles of fairness. This is not an easy matter, in part because of the diverse set of relevant equity principles are espoused and sometimes conflict, as for example, comparing the benefits principle with ability to pay a the local level and the many alternative burden-sharing principles for mitigating GHGs (see, e.g., Rose 2009).

9.4.3 Environmental Benefits

Climate change has placed a much stronger focus on the role of the environment in disasters than ever before. Previously only a very small portion of DRM had been oriented toward the environment. For example, a major study of the benefits of 10 years of U.S. FEMA hazard mitigation grants (MMC 2005; Rose et al. 2007) indicated that, while significant portion of the grants yielded environmental benefits, especially those associated with flood mitigation, less than 1 % of the total dollar benefits were environmental. The small fraction resulted despite the broad range of benefits, which included improved water quality (for recreational and commercial fishing, drinking water), reduction of hazardous wastes, and enhancement of wetlands, aesthetic, and health and safety benefits. In hardly any of the cases were environmental benefits cited as a major concern, but they were factored into the FEMA grant applications as Co-Benefits. At the same time, it should be mentioned that environmental benefits in the MMC study and others could very well be significantly under-estimated because of measurement difficulties in this realm.

In case of climate change, the environment is not only the medium through which the disaster is transmitted, but aspects of it are also among the major receptors of damage. Threatened on a much broader scale than ever before are delicate eco-systems, biodiversity, and soils, among others. Projected economic losses from climate change are in the hundreds of billions of dollars per year, with the sizable portion being environmental (IPCC 2014). Abatement of greenhouse gas emissions is being justified on the basis of all of these losses, and adaptation to climate change manifestations can further reduce losses. Most of the improved environmental areas are public goods or common property resources, but even still many of them are utilized by the private sector (e.g., river water for cooling nuclear power plants, pristine areas for recreation). Many environmental goods and services have private goods characteristics as well and are of course directly related to private sector interests. These include timber, soils, and biodiversity, which are threatened more than ever by surface temperature warming, drought, and increased wind and flood damage. In these cases, environmental services are direct benefits rather than Co-Benefits.

References

Aragón-Correa JA, Sharma S (2003) A contingent resource-based view of proactive corporate environmental strategy. Acad Manag Rev 28(1):71–88

Brugmann J (2012) Financing the resilient city. Environ Urban 24(1):215–232

Carrera A, Mesquita L, Perkins G, Vassolo R (2003) Business groups and their corporate strategies on the Argentine roller coaster competitive and anti-competitive shocks. Acad Manag Exec 17(3):32–44

Cutter S (2016) The landscape of disaster resilience indicators in the USA. Nat Hazards 80:741–758

Doh JP, Pearce JA (2004) Corporate entrepreneurship and real options in transitional policy environments: theory development. J Manag Stud 41(4):645–664

Federal Emergency Management Agency (FEMA) (2013) Multi-hazard loss estimation methodology (HAZUS®MH MR4). http://www.fema.gov/library/viewRecord.do?id=3726

Flores A, Smith A (2010) Surviving disasters. Wilf family department of politics. New York University, New York

Gigerenzer G, Selten R (eds) (2002) Bounded rationality: the adaptive toolbox. MIT Press, Cambridge, MA

Hallegatte S (2008) An adaptive regional input-output model and its application to the assessment of the economic cost of Katrina. Risk Anal 28(3):779–797

Hallegatte S (2016) Capturing co-benefits at the macro-economic scale. World Bank Policy Research Working Paper, Washington, DC

Hoffmann VH, Trautmann T, Hamprecht J (2009) Regulatory uncertainty: a reason to postpone investments? Not necessarily. J Manag Stud 46(7):645–664

Institute for Business and Home Safety (IBHS) (2015) FORTIFIED Program. http://www.smarthomeamerica.org

Intergovernmental Panel on Climate Change (IPCC) (2014) Fifth Assessment Report (AR5). Geneva

Kousky C (2012) Informing climate adaptation: a review of the economic costs of natural disasters, their determinants, and risk reduction options. Resources for the Future, Washington, DC

Kunreuther H (2006) Disaster mitigation and insurance: learning from Katrina. Ann Am Acad Pol Soc Sci 604:208–227

Kuneuther H, Michel-Kerjan E, Pauly M (2013) Making America more resilient toward natural disasters: a call for action. Environment 55(4):15–23

Multihazard Mitigation Council (MMC) (2005) Natural hazard mitigation saves: an independent study to assess the future savings from mitigation activities. Report to U.S. Congress on behalf of the National Institute of Building Sciences, Washington, DC

Overseas Development Institute (ODI) (2014) Case studies to support realising the resilience dividend. Climate and Environment Programme, ODI. London

Rose A (2009) The economics of climate change mitigation policy: international, national and regional perspectives. Edward Elgar, Cheltenham

Rose A (2014) Economic resilience and the sustainability of cities in the face of climate change: an ecological economics framework. In: Mazmanian D, Blanco H (eds) Handbook of sustainable cities. Edward Elgar, Cheltenham

Rose A (2015) Macroeconomic consequences of terrorist attacks: estimation for the analysis of policies and rules. In: Mansfield C, Smith VK (eds) Benefit transfer for the analysis of DHS policies and rules. Edward Elgar, Cheltenham

Rose A (2016) Capturing co-benefits of disaster risk management on the private sector side. World Bank Working Paper, Washington, DC.

Rose A, Porter K, Tierney K et al (2007) Benefit-cost analysis of FEMA hazard mitigation grant. Nat Hazards Rev 8(4):97–111

Rose A, Avetisyan M, Chatterjee S (2014) A framework for analyzing the economic tradeoffs between urban commerce and security. Risk Anal 14(8):1554–1579

Sheffi Y (2005) The resilient enterprise. MIT Press, Cambridge, MA

Surminski E, Tanner T (eds) (2016) Realising the triple resilience dividend: a new business case for disaster risk management. Springer, Heidelberg

Tanner T, Surminski S, Wilkinson E, Reid R, Rentshcler J, Rajput S (2015) The triple dividend of resilience: realizing development goals through the multiple benefits of disaster risk management. Overseas Development Institute, World Bank, London/Washington, DC

Vorhies F (2012) The economics of investing in disaster risk reduction. Working paper based on a review of the current literature commissioned by the Secretariat to the UN International Strategy for Disaster Reduction (UNISDR). Geneva.

Yang B, Burns M, Backhouse C (2004) Management of uncertainty through postponements. Int J Prod Res 42:1049–1064

Yoshida K, Deyle R (2005) Determinants of small business hazard mitigation. Nat Hazards Rev 6(1):1–12

Zolli A, Healy AM (2012) Resilience: why things bounce back. Free Press, New York

Chapter 10
Conclusion

While it is desirable to reduce disaster risk, this must be placed in the broader context of the risk equation, where Risk = (Threat X Vulnerability X Consequences). We can reduce the frequency and/or magnitude of many of these threats, we hence reduce vulnerability and consequences through pre-disaster mitigation. However, we can also reduce consequences via the static and dynamic resilience discussed above. Thus Resilience should be inserted on the equation.

It is important to balance the picture among the most cost-effective alternatives, both before and after the disaster strikes. It is also important to keep in mind that it is impossible to mitigate all threats. Resilience then becomes our next best line of defense against major disruptions to human development.

A key strategy is to translate ingenuity in coping with disasters in the short run into long-run decisions and practices that continuously promote sustainability. Resilience tactics to address resource shortages, such as conservation, input substitution, and technology modification, can be further refined for long-run application. Disasters can also provide opportunities for transitions to more sustainable paths in the reconstruction process through revised land-use planning, down-sizing, and industrial targeting, in addition to enhanced structural mitigation. Resilience offers many important lessons for sustainability. As noted by Zolli and Healy (2012), it places greater emphasis on flexibility and responding effectively to the realities of disequilibria, as opposed to unrealistically smooth equilibrium time-paths.

Following are some guideposts for implementing resilience in the short-term and transforming it into capacity that will promote sustainability in the long term:

- Identify effective resilience tactics at the micro, meso and macro levels based on actual experience. For example, ingenuity in conserving or substituting for critical resources under extreme stress should be examined for their more permanent potential under normal conditions.

A. Rose, *Defining and Measuring Economic Resilience from a Societal, Environmental and Security Perspective*, Integrated Disaster Risk Management,
DOI 10.1007/978-981-10-1533-5_10

- Develop resilience indicators based on evidence of successful practices and use them to monitor progress on resilience capacity. Even though disasters may be sporadic, the need to develop ways to mute their negative impacts should be a continuous process.
- Disseminate findings on best-practice resilience tactics and community response. Likewise, the continuous dissemination of information about resilience helps make it ingrained in daily life
- Evaluate the cost-effectiveness of resilience. This helps ensure resilience will be implemented as efficiently as possible, thereby helping to remain on or return to a sustainable path.
- Analyze the strategic tradeoffs between mitigation and resilience in terms of cost-effectiveness. Resilience should not be assessed in isolation of other major strategies, and the assessment should be done in terms of the ability to cope with short-run crises and to contribute to long-run sustainability.
- Identify ways to make resilience in the face of crises enduring, so as not to repeat previous mistakes. A good institutional memory contributes to both resilience and sustainability.
- Identify ways to transform short-run resilience responses into sustainability strategies. The view of resilience should go beyond consideration of individual tactics and should be evaluated in terms of broader community strategies that capture synergies
- Steer the economy and related systems to greater flexibility in terms of resource provision and utilization. A key attribute of resilience is flexibility, and ways need to be found to take advantage of this attribute, as in broadening the array of sustainable future paths.

The above list provides ways to make resilience experiences cumulative, so that progress continues. Overall, resilience empowers people to cope with threats to their security, livelihoods and overall well-being. Resilience has the potential to advance and deepen human progress in a sustainable manner. One way resilience can promote sustainability is to be more proactive than reactive. That is, rather than waiting for a crisis to take place, the emphasis should be on doing more planning for crises, as well as accumulating knowledge and capacities on a more enduring basis. This applies resilience not just to infrequent events, but to helping deal with long-term phenomena. Resilience, human development, and sustainability are closely intertwined.

I offer the following topics as priorities for future research:

1. *Measuring Static and Dynamic Economic Resilience in Practice*. To make prudent resource management decisions, one must consider the cost of each resilience tactic as well as its effectiveness. Very few studies have actually measured resilience in the aftermath of a disaster, and instead, analysts and policy makers have been overly dependent on simulation analysis. More survey and experimental research is needed.
2. *Identifying Obstacles to Resilience*. The simulation studies cited above are biased towards estimating resilience at its maximum effectiveness. This outcome is

unlikely due to the disarray accompanying most disasters, technical considerations, administrative obstacles, and limitations of decision-making. Research is needed on the extent of these obstacles and identifying ways to overcome them.

3. *Evaluating Inherent Resilience Potential.* It is important to identify resilience that is inherent in the survival mechanisms of businesses and households from those that require government policy assistance. Likewise more research is needed on the ability of markets to provide adequate price signals for resource allocation in a crisis. This way, future recovery efforts can better capitalize on existing capabilities and minimize duplication of government services.
4. *Incentives to Increase Resilience to Address Societal Needs.* Businesses increase resilience capacity for the sake of their own profits, but resilience often yields spillover benefits in the form of positive externalities and public goods that benefit others. More research is needed on how to induce decision-makers to address resilience from a broader perspective. This includes research on innovative risk financing and on traditional and innovative policy instruments.
5. *Compiling Resilience Indices Based on Actionable Variables.* Resilience is not just the flip-side of vulnerability. A resilience index is not only useful to study the recovery process, but also to improve it. This speaks to the importance of actionable variables. More research is needed to identify indicators that really matter to business decisions in the short-run.
6. *Equity and Environmental Justice.* Disasters typically hurt the poor and otherwise disadvantaged the most, because they are more vulnerable in the first place. These elements of society also have fewer resources to build resilience capacity, but, at the same time, resilience is relatively less expensive than other tactics to reduce losses. More research is needed on the potential of resilience to narrow the disparities of disaster impacts.

Reference

Zolli A, Healy AM (2012) Resilience: why things bounce back. Free Press, New York

MIX
Papier aus verantwortungsvollen Quellen
Paper from responsible sources
FSC® C105338

If you have any concerns about our products,
you can contact us on
ProductSafety@springernature.com

In case Publisher is established outside the EU,
the EU authorized representative is:
Springer Nature Customer Service Center GmbH
Europaplatz 3, 69115 Heidelberg, Germany

Printed by Libri Plureos GmbH
in Hamburg, Germany